The World According to Chuck

Stories about fathers, daughters, dogs, preachers, baseball, and sponge puppets.

CHUCK SIGARS

Copyright © 2004, 2010 by Chuck Sigars

All rights reserved. No part of this book may be reproduced or transmitted in any form or by any means, electronic or mechanical, including photocopying, recording, or by any information storage and retrieval system, without permission in writing by the copyright owner.

For my father, the Original Chuck.

CONTENTS

On Second Thought

1. Enter Laughing
2. A Moment for Mudville
3. The Boys'
4. Fall From Grace
5. Giving Thanks
6. Certain Unalienable Rights
7. A Day In The Life
8. Life With Father
9. A Winter's Tale
10. A Do-Over
11. Four Months and 13 Days
12. When All Else Fails
13. By The Content Of Their Character
14. If I Had A Hammer
15. Home Alone
16. The Little Church That Could
17. March Madness
18. Justice For All
19. The Inside-Out Boy
20. Over The Rainbow
21. The Lion, The Witch, and The Other Witch
22. Memories of the Monte Vista Hotel
23. Men Don't Leave
24. A Beautiful Day In The Neighborhood
25. On The Road
26. Do Not Pass "Go"
27. The Stuff That Dreams Are Made Of
28. The Other Chuck
29. A Dumb Blond Joke
30. The Measure Of A Man
31. The First Day
32. Try To Remember
33. Suffer The Little Children
34. And The Winner Is...
35. A Message For Mrs. Kurtenbach
36. Evil In Our Mists
37. It Is Right To Give Our Thanks and Praise
38. Keeping The Faith

39. The Best Christmas Ever
40. Teach Your Children Well
41. The Civics Lesson
42. Chicken Soup For The Soul
43. The Right Stuff
44. What Have I Got To Lose? (don't answer)
45. Angels Among Us
46. Springtime For Somebody, Somewhere
47. Real Men Don't Floss
48. Truth, Justice, and the American Way. Or Else
49. Lost and Found
50. Report From The Front. And Back. And Sides
51. The Dance Lesson
52. Becoming Moe
53. The Prophecy
54. Mars and Venus
55. School Daze
56. The Leader of the Band
57. Alpha and Omega
58. Harry and Where The Heart Is
59. Mary and Madelynne
60. Freedom's Just Another Word For...
61. Chasing Chevy
62. Schnebley Hill Road
63. The Boys of Summer
64. Preachers I Know
65. Bethy Was Here
66. In Lieu of Flowers
67. The Boy On Elm Street
68. Witness
69. Father to the Man
70. Gen-U-flection
71. It's A Zoo Out There
72. The Rummage Sale
73. Thank Heaven...
74. The Message
75. The Quality of Mercy
76. One Particular Spring
77. This Perfect Day

On Second Thought

At first, I just thought I would write some jokes.

When I began writing for the Mukilteo Beacon in October 2001, that was the plan. Make some jokes, poke some fun at myself and my family, note some current events and otherwise keep it light.

In retrospect, I suppose the proximity of Sept. 11 to my start as a weekly columnist should have been a clue that this might be an eventful experience, writing about my world.

The first edition of <u>The World According to Chuck</u> was published in 2004. On looking back at what turned out to be essentially a printed file cabinet, containing not just columns but blog posts, essays for the Seattle Times, notes to myself and I think at least a couple of recipes, it occurred to me that I wanted a do-over.

This, then, is what we have: Three years of life, all published in the Beacon, and in chronological order, from my search for laughter in the post-9/11 culture to Randy Johnson's perfect game. There are some jokes, funny or not, but also observations on what happens when you're busy writing a weekly column.

That would be, as it turns out, life, and death, passages and maybe a couple of prophecies.

It's all mine, though.

Chuck Sigars. December 2010

Enter Laughing

I'd like to pose an empirical question today. As you know, empiricism was invented by ancient Greek philosophers, who asked "If a tree falls in the forest and no one is there, does it make a sound?", from which we derive the popular phrase, "Get a life." Empirical, of course, is a very old word that comes from the Latin imperator, from which we get the term "emperor", which in turn can be traced to the classic fable The Emperor's New Clothes and so essentially is defined as "Something that if you can't see it or hear it, ain't there, unless you're ignorant, and then maybe it is."

Okay, so I made that up. Just a little joke.

Which brings up my empirical question. After the events of September 11th, as we're still in the midst of national mourning and shock and anger, I wonder: If something comical happens, and an entire country has temporarily lost its sense of humor...is it still funny?

But I wonder a lot these days. It seems I'm not alone, either. Lots of questioning is going on out there, I suspect, and it runs a little deeper than what to cook for dinner or whom to vote for or whether or not the Seahawks will go to the Super Bowl in our lifetime. I'm nowhere near the best judge; I don't travel at all, my circle of friends and acquaintances is small and cozy, and I don't listen to talk radio because of my blood pressure thing. But I work at home and so I like to get out to the grocery store just to be around people, and I notice something that makes me uncomfortable.

Not a lot of laughter out there. Not a lot of smiles or joking with the checker or self-deprecating humor about not looking where you're going with your cart or how the kids just have to have this brand of macaroni and cheese. It's pretty business-like and solemn, and oh how I wish I could hear a little laughter in the aisles. I wish that a lot.

British playwright Harold Pinter, who since the 1950s has been writing hilarious plays about dark subjects, was once asked to give his definition of the difference between tragedy and comedy. "Everything is comedy," he answered. "The thing about tragedy is, it's just not funny anymore."

Politics, sports, religion: You name it, somebody's making jokes about it. There hasn't been a disaster of some sort in recent memory that hasn't spurred someone to pass around a sick joke about it.. With the advent of the internet, these fly out at the speed of light to forwarded lists of friends and we see them and feel bad about laughing. But not this time. This is too serious. This time it struck home, and it's just not funny anymore.

Things change. But some don't. And as we grieve, worry, prepare, and adjust to a changing and changed world, I would hope that we'd look at our lives and find them funny again, from time to time. Not to prevent the terrorists from winning, not to keep things normal for the kids, not even to keep from weeping...but because it's so essentially human. We like to say that our ability to reason, our big brain, separates us from the other creatures on this planet. Okay, maybe. On the other hand,

I have a feeling that a lot of us have either owned or known a dog, for example, that was smarter than at least a couple of our cousins. But dogs don't laugh.

And we do. A famous quote from 1963 comes to mind. After President Kennedy was assassinated, columnist Mary McGrory said to Patrick Moynihan, "We'll never laugh again." To which Moynihan replied, "Mary, we'll laugh again. We'll just never be young again."

We're going to be different, no question. And yeah, we're a little sensitive right now. Ask Bill Maher. Ask David Letterman and Jon Stewart, both based in New York, who started their first shows back after the terrorist attacks with long, awkward, touching personal statements. Then they got around to their jobs of trying to make us laugh. God love 'em for that, I say.

We may not feel as safe as we did, but we'll manage. Life may not be as convenient as it was, but we'll deal with it. The world may seem scarier to us...but sure, we'll laugh again. We always have, and we should. Soon.

I think, by the way, that the Seahawks will go to a Super Bowl in my lifetime. Call me an optimist. Call me crazy. Go ahead, laugh.

I like the sound of that.

A Moment For Mudville

I'm the eternal optimist. Always have been. The glass is always half full, the sun always rises, it ain't over until—

Okay. Sorry. It's over. No more Mariners. Must have been daydreaming there.

I love baseball. I know there are lots of you out there who don't. Some of you have absolutely no interest in baseball or sports at all, and might even wonder a bit about those of us who do.

Especially now, when we have troops in Afghanistan and rubble in New York. There are more important things. It's just a game, after all. I have no desire to be poetic or reverent about it. I don't think it's the cure for what ails you, or a metaphor for life, or the answer to national turmoil.

Well, sometimes I think it's a metaphor for life. And I really like "Casey At The Bat." But that's all.

I'm just a little surprised by some of the bitterness in the last week or so. We're disappointed, sure, but Northwest sports fans have always enjoyed a strange equation that lets a few spectacular moments equal years of frustration. So why this year has the process, the journey, become meaningless because it didn't end in...what? A T-shirt with "Champions" across it? I don't think they hand out rings to the fans. And the season would still be over.

We've been Mariners fans in my house for a long time. It's a constant from April through October. The radio or TV is always on, our conversations are speckled with stats and commentary, the voices of Dave and Rick are background to our lives. There's an warm familiarity to it. If an man from Mars or somebody from Nebraska, say, were to listen in as we talk, they might assume Lou is our temperamental neighbor and Jay is the kid down the street and Edgar is our cat.

Six months, 162 games. Which means I can listen to or watch most games and not mind much if we lose. It's a gentle humming; elevator music for long summer days to accompany lawn mowing or garage cleaning. It's something I can share with strangers and friends, my wife and neighbors.

It's just a game. A game in which there's always a last chance, a final hope, and no clock to sweat over. A game played by incredible physical specimens, but also by short guys and slow guys and old guys and even fat guys (I love that part). A famous ballplayer was caught smoking a cigarette by a fan, and she chastised him. "You're supposed to be an athlete," she said. "Lady, I'm not an athlete," he replied. "I'm a baseball player."

It's a game that requires heightened reflexes, excellent eyesight, speed, strength, stamina, and cunning, but not all at once and not all in one guy. There's little grandstanding in baseball, because someone on the bench is usually better at something than you are. Like running. Pitchers almost seven feet tall rely on 5'7" shortstops to cover for their mistakes. Managers wear the same uniforms as the players they lead. It's a game about community, about depending on one another, about overcoming your limitations and knowing what they are at the same time. It's just a game, but it's a great game.

And this season we watched it played by a great team. I've heard the pronouncements: The 2001 Mariners will be ridiculed because they won 116 games in the regular season and then choked in the playoffs. They'll go down in history as The Little Team That Couldn't. Ask me if I care.

I'll never be the ultimate fan. My life is too busy to collect autographs and scorecards and stand in line 48 hours for playoff tickets. But for half a year I basked in the glow of a team that played baseball with almost mathematical symmetry: Get the lead-off man on, bunt him to second, double him home. Occasionally lift one into the upper deck for old times' sake, but generally keep the ball in the park where it can be thrown and caught and muffed and missed, and one run scores and then another. And it seemed they won every game.

I know it's trivial and insignificant in The Big Picture. I know people are dead and people are grieving, and a bat hitting a ball isn't important. But joy is, and sometimes in a complicated world we find joy in trivial and insignificant things. A stolen base. A perfect bunt. A sunny afternoon in July, with the Mariners with a 20-game lead, Ichiro on second and Edgar at the plate with a 2 and 0 count, when nothing seems impossible and everyone is smiling and for a short time all our troubles just fly, fly away.

The Boys

On my desk sits a picture of four men. They appear to be on a beach. They look cold. They also appear to be getting on up there in years, which is sort of a shock considering one of them is me.

This was taken on the Oregon coast last July, so I've pretty much recovered by now, although I still have the occasional bad dream. I mean, how would you like to spend time with a group of people who are determined to remind you of every mistake you ever made, every youthful indiscretion, every wrong move, every dumb thing you ever did? Over and over again. Sounds like a "Twilight Zone" episode, doesn't it?

I do this every summer.

It started at Maryvale High School in Phoenix. My brother, Bill, met Randy in the spring of 1973 in shop class. I met Randy the next fall in biology class. Randy and Dave met in health class. Bill met Dave through me. I met Dave through Randy. My brother and I go way back, of course. And somehow, over the years, this complex web of interpersonal relationships turned into a quartet of guys who every summer take a weekend expecting to have fun and ending up mostly with indigestion, then do it again the next year. And they say pigeons are stupid.

It started as The Annual Camping Trip. Or, as we ended up referring to it, The Annual (supply rude word of your choice here) Camping Trip. One time it rained the entire time and we slept in Dave's Volkswagen. One time we couldn't get a fire started. One time Randy had discovered a love of fishing so the rest of us had loads of fun watching him do that.

One time we got separated while inner tubing down the Salt River and Randy spent eight hours wandering around dressed only in gym shorts while the rest of us attempted to traverse rapids at midnight and we saw a UFO and I saved Bill's life, although he won't admit this, and we finally found Randy in the backseat of a park ranger's car and he refused to speak to the rest of us for months.

Stuff like that. Beer was usually involved, too.

It's been a spotty tradition. We pretty much missed our 30s, what with me moving to Washington and Bill having lots of kids and Dave getting interested in really strange music and Randy marrying a deranged woman who refused to let him leave the house. Seriously. I'm not kidding.

But now, settled somewhat in our 40s, three of us living in the Northwest and one still in Phoenix but with a pathological desire to get out of the house, we make our annual trek, usually to somewhere in Oregon, and hang out for a weekend.

We talk. We wander around, try to find the best chicken wings in a particular town, argue about music and politics and bluntly discuss who has the least hair (Dave) and who has gained the most weight (me) and who is the shortest (Bill, hands down) and who married the craziest woman (guess). And there's lots of "Remember when..." and lots of laughter and lots of coffee in the mornings. Beer is still involved. And Randy always gets gas from the chicken wings and we make him stay outside for a while. Then we pack up and head for the airport or the highway and no one says much.

Maybe there's some sort of genetic imperative that drives four middle-aged guys to the Oregon coast every summer to eat bad food and re-hash old grievances and memories and share one bathroom. And trust me: One bathroom is really, really not enough.

My wife is a graduate student these days and knows a whole lot about traditions and rituals, but when I get home from these weekends she just says, "I'm glad you're still alive," so I wonder. But not that much.

We go because we've known each other since we were kids and had hair down to our shoulders and actual waistlines.

We go because if we're out walking in the sand and one of us stops and says, "You know what? Life is sort of like a beach" we can hold his head under water until he promises not to ever, ever say something that stupid again, and there are no hard feelings.

We go because we like each other, because we have a good time generally, because life is complicated and friends are few and we know where all the bodies are buried, so to speak.

Or maybe it's just the chicken wings. Hard to say. Anyway, I'm going next year. Who am I to mess with tradition?

Besides, Randy really needs to get out once in awhile.

Fall From Grace

An anniversary comes up in a couple of days. It's not exactly the occasion that inspires a party, but I'm up for one in case anybody is interested. Money is always a nice gift, by the way.

Before we go much further, I want to say that I'm going to be talking a lot about a part of my anatomy. There's nothing wrong with this part, and in fact we all have this part, and there are many mild euphemisms I could use in a family newspaper for this part. But those strike me as being condescending to a mature and intelligent readership, and a little childish and cutesy. So I'm just going to use correct terminology and refer to it as my "lulu."

I've worked in my home office in the basement now for almost 13 years. I went into Seattle one morning in 1989 and cleaned out my desk, and then I drove home and made French toast for my 4-year-old daughter. I told her that daddy was going to be working at home from now on, and that I could make her French toast every day. Showing a healthy skepticism even then, she was less than thrilled. Probably she thought that if this big change in our lives meant she would have to eat the same thing for breakfast the rest of her life, she couldn't get all that excited.

But I was home. I avoided a commute and road rage. No possibility of an irate employee entering my office with an automatic weapon. I didn't even have to wear real pants. I could just sit on my "lulu" in front of the computer and work. I thought I was safe.

I thought that until November 17th, 2000, when I headed downstairs to the basement and made a slight mistake. That being, I slipped and fell and bumped on my "lulu" down several steps, thereby demonstrating Newton's first law that an object in motion will stay in motion until it reaches the bottom of the stairs, at which time it will rise up and say a lot of bad words.

I broke my tailbone. My coccyx. This little vestigial portion of the spine that ends about where your "lulu" begins. It's left over from when we had tails, if you accept that, or else just one of God's little jokes, like eyebrows and the appendix and William Shatner.

So what happens is the coccyx now swings a lot (which apparently coccyxes like to do) whenever you sit or stand up from sitting. This sends a message to the brain, which apparently disapproves of swinging and therefore causes the area around your "lulu" to hurt very, very much, and you squirm and use expressions you haven't since you started having kids. This is real embarrassing in church.

There's not even an outward sign like a cast or a sling. I can't hang my head a little sheepishly and say, "Yeah, me and Frank was trying to run some conduit and I reached up to hand him a grouter with a 5/16ths drill bit and I rammed my shoulder into a beveled delaminator."

I've done it all, too. Physical therapy. Multiple consultations. Drugs that would make me an instant friend of Robert Downey,

Jr. I had steroids injected directly into my tailbone, which was performed in a small room with three nurses hovering around as my bare "lulu" lay exposed to the world, and I could actually watch via fluoroscopy as a needle approximately three feet long was slid very slooowly into my spine. And I'm making it sound more pleasant than it was.

And people are so kind. They mean well. They come up to me and say, "So, how's the, uh...I mean, how is...y'know..." I want to scream, "THE WORD IS 'LULU!' JUST SAY IT!"

So, it's a year now. And I'm better, really. Just as modern science discovered a blood pressure medication would grow hair on the back of your head, now a drug intended to prevent seizures has been shown to be effective in chronic pain, without the side effects of narcotics (such as finding episodes of "This Old House" suddenly hilarious).

I'd like to say thanks to Dr. Ann Dryer at The Everett Clinic, who is my family physician and has helped me tremendously during this ordeal by being sympathetic and understanding and thoughtfully covering her mouth discreetly at those times when the image of an overweight, middle-aged man falling on his "lulu" becomes just too funny. I'd also like to tell her that I finally figured out that when mumbled, the words "My coccyx" sound remarkably like "My car accident", which explains some of her nurses' chart entries.

This would never happen, of course, if we would just use the correct terminology.

Giving Thanks

I love Thanksgiving. I always have, ever since I was a kid. It's way better than Christmas. Once the presents are opened Christmas fades quickly, but turkey sandwiches can last a week or more if you're careful.

Here in the Sigars household, Thanksgiving season usually starts the week before, officially begun when my wife says, "OHMYGOD, MY PARENTS WILL BE HERE IN TWO DAYS AND THERE'S MOLD GROWING ON THE COUCH!" And so we all pitch in, and while I love my in-laws and always enjoy their visits, clean bathrooms are a special treat, too.

We're pretty traditional, with a big turkey and dressing and pies and a lot of stuff I eat even though I'm not sure exactly what it is. We say grace and talk about what we're thankful for, and we watch the Cowboys play. My in-laws are Texans, and on Thanksgiving we're all Dallas fans.

Once, in 1986, we had Thanksgiving in Texas and the Cowboys were playing the Seahawks, and to our horror the Hawks won. Just creamed them. And while my wife's family was polite and said nice things about the game, I remember we had to hitch a ride to the airport and didn't get Christmas cards from them for a couple of years. Texans take their football very seriously.

Food, football, and family. And I have a lot to be thankful for, as always. But just now, as I was sitting at the computer here thinking about Thanksgiving, I noticed something that reminded me how complicated gratitude can be sometimes.

When I was a kid, I loved to go visit my Grandma Baker. She'd always give me paper and pencil and I'd sit at her kitchen table and write stuff. When I got a bit older she'd let me use her typewriter, and I'd peck out stories about Batman or Daniel Boone or whatever my latest television-inspired interest was.

One day, when I was on a Zorro kick, I sat down and began an involved, complicated plot that as I recall involved a train robbery and a kidnapping and lots of sword fights and possibly time travel. My typing skills were pretty primitive, of course, and when my parents announced it was time to go, I was only a quarter of the way through my story and just coming to the good part, and I burst into tears.

Grandma stepped in. She told my folks she'd take me home later, and she fed me a nice dinner and then sat down at the typewriter and had me dictate my Zorro story to her as she typed it.

I should note that my grandmother was a complicated person. She'd led a pretty rough life, and could be an opinionated and sharp-tongued woman at times. As I grew older she made me uncomfortable and I tried to avoid her. This was a rotten thing to do but I did it, and I hurt her feelings a lot.

Once, when I was about 25, I'd been thoughtless once again to Grandma and I wrote her a letter. I apologized, and I thanked her for that time when I was a kid. She wrote back, telling me that of course she forgave me, that she remembered the Zorro thing too, and that she thought sometimes the two of us just didn't understand each other. This was a gracious thing to say, and true enough, I guess.

She's been gone quite a while now, but my dad's stepfather died only two years ago. As my parents went about the chore of straightening his affairs, they found that he had kept almost everything he and my grandmother had accumulated over the years. As things were disposed of, they asked if any of the kids wanted something as a keepsake before they sold it or gave it away.

So now, on my desk, sits a gray 1955 Remington manual typewriter. As I work at the computer it's visible in the corner of my eye. If I squint a little, I can almost see an 8-year-old boy hunched over the keyboard, slowly typing his stories. I keep it there to remind me how a single act of kindness can resonate over the years. It's a good thing to remember.

I'm glad I thanked her. It occurred to me today, though, that sometimes being grateful comes with responsibility, even if it's subtle. Sometimes it's just accepting our good fortune and being aware of those who have less. Sometimes it's about passing a good deed along to someone else. And sometimes it's about debt, and implied promises.

As she drove me home that night, my grandma told me that I was a good little writer, and that she was sure someday I would write something just for her.

I can't tell you how sorry I am that it took this long.

Certain Unalienable Rights

Soon after September 11th, as you may recall, Rev. Jerry Falwell informed us that he knew who was responsible for the attacks. According to the good reverend, this included gays, the ACLU, and feminists. This came as a surprise to most of us, of course, as we were sort of suspecting terrorists. Just goes to show you how ignorant we can be.

I mention this because my wife is a feminist, and she refuses to accept any responsibility at all. She won't own up to her part in the moral decline of our nation. Can you believe this? And she calls herself an American.

But then, a lot of different people claim to be Americans. A few days after the events of September 11th, a man in Mesa, Arizona, shot and killed the owner of a small convenience store, who happened to be from India. By all accounts, the victim was a man who loved children and went out of his way to be a good neighbor. He wore a turban of sorts, and I guess that was enough for his murderer, who when arrested seemed astonished and kept saying, "But I'm a REAL American!"

A real stupid American, of course, since even if he assumed these attacks were planned and carried out by the entire population of Afghanistan, he was off by two countries. But, hey, the guy wore a turban.

I know, Falwell recanted sort of and apologized. And I know he has a tendency to be something of a jerk anyway. But I don't think he's the only one who wants to place blame on people who have different ideas or different behavior, who dress or appear somehow strange. There are now people in our own community who are afraid to go outside in traditional Muslim dress for fear of some moron with a gun. So I guess we're guaranteed life, liberty, and the pursuit of happiness, but only if we wear politically correct clothing. Does the word "Taliban" suddenly come up?

We have a long history in this country of looking for the bogeyman (bogeyperson? I need to ask my wife). There's always been an undercurrent of intolerance running through American history, even as we've built a diverse population and solidified equal rights in legislation. You might even call it sort of a flaw in the American character. Maybe people in other countries find it endearing or sort of charming, I don't know. Those wacky Americans, they're always hating somebody or other.

For a while, I thought it was going to settle down when it seemed like all the people who were angry could just pick on Bill Clinton, but it hasn't stopped. Talk radio has largely turned from people who wanted to relate their alien abductions to rants about liberals or gun owners or gays or Christians. And we've now been given so many niche outlets to indulge our particular dislikes that a lot of people, at least many I've run across, seem honestly astonished to learn that someone who looks like them and lives in their neighborhood might actually disagree with their opinion.

America is hard to do. Take a whole mess of land, rich with natural resources, plop down some first-rate 18th century intellectuals to carve out a Constitution unparalleled in human history, get some hardy types to work the land and push the frontiers, then open the borders and say come, we've got plenty of room. And they do, all types and beliefs and practices. Despite the poetic image, we're not a melting pot; we're not a homogeneous society and never have been. We're a smorgasbord of humankind, an eclectic collection of dreamers and doers. We bicker and squabble as people do, but somehow there's an American alchemy that produces amazing results.

It's easy in stressful times to forget, or refuse to accept, that our diversity makes us great, that our very differences fuel this wonderful American experiment. It's easy to ignore the enormous contributions that people of all colors and faiths and cultures and behaviors make in our lives. It's easy to look for the scapegoats, to make jokes about odd-sounding names and to harass people who look or think differently. It's easy to look for imagined enemies within, and thereby ignore the real ones. Which is what they want, by the way.

A feminist, according to the dictionary (for the benefit of Jerry), is someone who espouses social, economic, and political equality of the sexes. Which describes my wife pretty well. It also describes me. And it describes the current President of the United States, at least by his words and actions. I'm pretty sure we're all real Americans.

On the other hand, Osama bin Laden is definitely not a feminist. I doubt he's all that fond of gays or the ACLU, either. I don't know how he feels about turbans. But different strokes...

A Day In The Life

I don't exactly bound out of bed on my best days, but this one is slow. Painful, even. I've got a bad cold that's lingering like the last guest at a good party. My immune system is shot, no doubt. When was the last time I ate an orange, I wonder. I sneeze a few times on my way downstairs, tea in hand. Not a good start.

Is it me, or is it grayer than usual these days? I open the blinds and I feel as though I'm staring at a 1940s film Ted Turner never got around to colorizing. No wonder I'm thinking in bad Raymond Chandler prose. Lots of dark, heavy clouds. I wouldn't want to fly in this weather. I'm not sure I really want to live in it. Maybe I need to get some of those bright lights for my office.

I log online, which seems to take longer every day, and I see it right away. I read the news today oh boy. George Harrison, dead at 58 from cancer. I take this in slowly, trying to clear my cobwebs. George Harrison is dead. The youngest. The most spiritual, probably the best musician of the bunch. Quiet, but only sometimes. At their first recording session, producer George Martin said, "Tell me if there's anything you don't like." Harrison spoke up. "First of all, I don't like your tie," he said. Words are everything, be careful, he seems to say.

I went with my brother one day when he bought a Beatles record. He got it in a grocery store, for some reason. The checker held up the album. "I've never heard of any of these songs," he sneered and I felt embarrassed but I distinctly remember thinking, "You will, though, you jerk" and I was right. I was probably 9 years old but I've always remembered that day. I remembered it the first time I heard "Yesterday" condensed into Muzak somewhere. Yeah, you will.

I can't get my office warm. My fingers are stiff on the keyboard, and I can't concentrate on work, and I really, really need to. Think about it later, I say to myself, then I remember my grandmother saying that she cried like a baby when Elvis died. My grandmother. These little notches we make, marking how our world changes when somebody we don't know but liked or admired or watched or listened to is gone.

I take a break and go to the store with my son. In the car I ask him if he knows The Beatles. "Yeah, they're cool," he says, and when I tell him the news he sighs and says, "Everybody's dying these days" and I have no idea what he's talking about. Or maybe I do. I wonder if when he's my age he'll log on or turn on or whatever he does to get his daily information and hear something. I dunno, Robin Williams has died, something. And he'll think, "He was my favorite actor when I was a kid" and his day will be different.

The store is crowded and everyone looks glum to me. Oh, look at all the lonely people. John stops half a dozen times to ask for something he sees on the shelf and I'm irritated. A guy my age watches this and says, "I hate bringing the kids with me" and as he passes I notice he's humming "My Sweet Lord." And it's raining as I leave.

What difference does it make, I think, but it does. And the wind is now kicking up and the lights are flickering. It's been a long cold lonely winter. I should watch the news but retrospectives are not what I have in mind, and I put in a Beatles CD instead. Early stuff, 1965 or so, ersatz Buddy Holly really but with that sweet harmony.

I think of a documentary I saw when The Fab Four played a command performance. They launched into "Twist and Shout" and the camera focused on the Queen and I swear she looked like she was about to get up and boogie in the aisles.

I'm starting to feel better. I sit back and listen. It hasn't been such a bad day. And though the news was very sad. Wistful maybe, but a reminder that our lives are touched by strangers all the time. Good ones, bad ones. Some of them hang around. Some of them change us a bit. Some of them make music.

The weather report says we could get some clearing tomorrow. I may boogie myself. Funny how simple things make a difference. Just when life is looking pretty bleak, here comes the sun.

Life With Father

This year, December 14th falls on a Friday. It does that every once in a while. You'd think it would be every seven years, but you'd be wrong. This has to do with Leap Year or Daylight Savings Time or something.

It fell on a Friday in 1984, too. I remember. I was in the kitchen preparing my favorite dinner, tacos and beer, which was about the extent of my cooking skills. I was browning ground beef and opening can #2, when my wife came out of the bathroom with an odd look on her face and said, "Don't drink any more beer."

She says this all the time, of course, but, again, she had an odd look on her face. She would actually make a lot of faces over the next 12 hours, many of which I hesitate to describe, but the next morning I watched the sun rise over downtown Seattle from a window in Swedish Hospital, holding in my arms my newborn daughter. A few weeks earlier than expected, but healthy and beautiful. I was 26 years old. It was the best day of my life.

A couple of minutes after Beth was born, I ran and grabbed the video camera and pretty much didn't put it down for about five years. I began to organize the tapes: Beth Volume I, Volume II, etc. And this was in the first week. I had a three-tape set entitled "Beth Sleeping." One afternoon I turned the camera on and a few minutes later she haltingly walked from one chair to another on her own; her first steps. I'm pretty sure I made tacos that night.

My wife and I were opposed to day care, based on the sound principle that we couldn't afford it, so we worked a lot of odd shifts to balance the parenting. I usually got the late mornings and early afternoons. For several years of my life, then, I spent most of my non-working time with a little girl.

I had a tendency to play Mr. Rogers. I took her to the library. I used apples and oranges to demonstrate how the earth moves around the sun. I taught her about syllogisms and syntax. We spent hours playing "Answer Girl," a game we made up in which I'd quiz her on numbers and colors and TV show theme songs.

She was bright and curious and only occasionally cynical, as when she saw "Peter Pan" for the first time. "No one can lose their shadow," she said disdainfully, and turned off the TV. This was pure Beth.

Not that I want to be too sentimental about a time of very little sleep and endless hours of Big Bird. I wasn't all that far removed from the freedom of my college days not to realize I had been pretty neatly tied around a little finger.

If there was a song on the radio she particularly liked, Beth would instruct me to get down on one knee and she would jump and wrap her arms around my neck, and I'd lift her up and we'd dance around the living room. Who am I, Bojangles?, I'd think, wondering whether I should have closed the shades first.

Then, of course, one day I drove her to school and she flipped down the visor to check her hair in the mirror, and that was pretty much that. The little girl whose highlight of the day used to be watching me shave had other things to do. My duties had been reduced to handing over cash and jump starting her car.

Beth will spend her 17th birthday following in her mother's musical footsteps, earning a few bucks playing the cello with her group, Trionfare Trio, at a holiday gig (there's your plug, guys). My cooking skills have improved, but maybe I'll make tacos anyway. Just to feel useful; for it suddenly occurs to me that out of all the things I know how to do, after all the childhood fantasies of becoming a wide receiver or a movie star, it turns out the thing that came most naturally to me was being the father of a little girl. And now my time is up.

So maybe I can be excused a moment or two of nostalgia. Maybe I can be forgiven for wondering when that very last game of Answer Girl was. Maybe you can understand how, from time to time, I have the oddest feeling that I've somehow lost my shadow.

It's there, though, somewhere. It lingers on lazy afternoons in a small apartment with a red-haired 3-year-old girl. She holds on tightly and we dance around the living room, and for a few hours I am her entire universe, and she is mine.

A Winter's Tale

I usually sleep soundly. Audibly soundly, according to my wife. And my neighbors. Occasionally the seismic laboratory at the UW.

But not this Christmas Eve, for some reason. Maybe I heard something. Maybe it was the rum balls. I stayed in bed for a while, then finally got up and walked into the kitchen to get a glass of milk. I heard a rustling in the living room and figured the dog was sniffing the presents under the tree, so I went in and that's when I saw him.

He looked just like the pictures. Big guy, round face, familiar flashy costume.

Are some of you thinking it was Elvis? It wasn't Elvis.

Father Christmas. Mr. C. The original Nick At Night. He was bent over under the tree but straightened up right away. If he had a twinkle in his eye, he'd left it at home. All I saw was weariness and a bit of suspicion. We just stared at each other for a while. "You, um, brought me a bike once," I finally croaked out.

He shifted his weight a little, sighed, and said, "I bring a lot of bikes." There was more silence, so I added, "It was green." I swear he rolled his eyes a bit. "Oh, yeah, the green one," he muttered and I felt like a fool.

He went over to the recliner and sat down with a groan. "I'm beat," he said, rubbing his neck. Then he gestured toward the fireplace. "You planning on cleaning that chimney one of these days?" he asked. I murmured something about getting around to it soon, and he sighed again. "Make sure you get a professional," he said.

I can't explain it. Maybe he just needed to rest. Maybe it was because I didn't tie him up and call a tabloid to come take his picture. At any rate, we talked some. I made him a sandwich. We chatted about the weather. He took his boots off and rubbed his feet. I asked him if the heightened security had affected him this year. He waved his hand, almost nonchalantly and sad at the same time. "There've always been wars somewhere," he said.

He pulled out his pipe and lit it. Normally no one smokes in my house unless my dad comes for a visit, but I figured I'd find a way to explain it to my wife. It had a nice smell, actually; sort of peppermint. He looked around at some of the pictures we've got on the walls and commented on how the kids have grown. We talked a little about the Mariners. I thought about the hours I'd spent in the last couple of weeks in stores, trying to find the right gifts. "What did the kids want this year?" I asked. "I mean, the number one item. Not just here, but worldwide. What's the big wish?"

His face changed briefly and then it was gone, but for that moment he looked old. Real old. He puffed on his pipe. "Food," he finally said. "The big wish is food."

It was awkward. I thought about the feast we would have in a few hours. It's been a rough year for us, but still. The freezer was full. No one was going to miss a meal, even though some of us probably could stand to. "You have no idea," he said, "How many kids are hungry tonight." I had an idea. "Millions," I offered. He gave me that look again, the old one. "Try a billion," he said.

"And parents," he added. "A lot of them want their parents back. AIDS in Africa. War in the Middle East. Afghanistan. New York. Lots in New York." He stood up. "And I'm just one man," he said.

I have little use for guilt. It leads to self pity, and that gets in the way of fixing problems. I felt obligated to state my case. "I'm also just one man," I said. And for the first time he smiled. "Then that makes two of us," he said.

"You watch the towers collapse and then you fill up your gas-guzzling SUV. Money that goes into the pockets of those who sponsor the terrorists. You spend hours watching TV that could be spent working in a shelter or food bank. You think you're just one guy? Then find some more."

And then he was gone. I could have shifted my eyes for a second; I dunno. He was just gone. I ran to the door and walked out on the front deck. It was clear and cold, but I saw no reindeer.

Then again, there are lots of things I've never seen. Doesn't mean they don't exist. I finally went back inside where it was warm. Never got back to sleep, though.

A Do-Over

There's just something about January 1st. Whether we make resolutions or not, it's a blank calendar waiting to be filled with different stuff. Changes, new ideas, second chances. Second chances in particular, at least to me. I've always been fond of that concept.

An actor friend of mine once told the story of when he was young and trying to break into show business. He managed to land a job walking the dog of a famous entertainer. One day in the park, this dog spotted a squirrel, pulled loose from my friend's hand, and ran off. He searched for hours without success, and then slunk home, too terrified to face the owner, sure he had blown his big chance.

He hadn't, as it turns out, but I remember those feelings, how every big mistake seems irreversible and terminal when you're young and lack the perspective of a few more years. And how you wonder if you'll ever get a second chance.

My friend, as it turned out, gave me one.

When I was 15, I had this idea I wanted to be a stand-up comic. I took it seriously. I spent many nights in front of the TV with a small audio cassette recorder, taping comedians on Johnny Carson. I studied funny people from Fred Allen to Freddie Prinze. I tried out routines and impressions on my family for hours until they started making ugly threats. I was convinced I just needed my Big Break.

I got it in the spring of my sophomore year in high school. A benefit show was being held in my home town, and they'd managed to snag a celebrity who lived in the area to act as producer and emcee. Auditions were to be held on a Saturday, and they were going to use local talent, professional or otherwise.

I honed my act down to a tight five minutes with a big finish, a take-off on the then-popular "Columbo" show, and showed up bright and early. And waited. Apparently I wasn't the only one with a dream. Singers, dancers, mimes, magicians, actors, jugglers...you name it, they were there, most of them ahead of me. By late afternoon they were stopped after a minute or so with a "Thank you, next please."

As I said, I was 15. I had no idea how to cut my act quickly, so when I finally got onstage I just started from the beginning. Sure enough, sixty seconds into it I got a tug on my arm and a "Thank you." I had blown my big opportunity.

My show biz ambitions ended years ago, mostly because I had no stomach for the self promotion and aggressiveness it requires (something about limited talent should go here, too). So I have no explanation for what happened next. I pulled away from the lady trying to escort me offstage, leaned into the mike and looked down at the poor celebrity they'd roped into doing this show.

He held a clipboard in his lap, and after eight-plus hours of judging acts he looked tired. "Please let me do my Columbo bit," I begged. He smiled a little. "OK, let him do Columbo." So I did. And he cast me.

This was my friend. "Friend" is not really accurate. I knew him for a brief period a long time ago. It would be a safe bet that he has no memory of me whatsoever. I remember him, though. He was a very nice man and good natured. I was the youngest performer in the show, so he took a little extra time with me. He gave me a few suggestions for my act. He told the story of the dog. He was distant in the way a busy person is, the way a shy person is, but he was accessible and friendly. I liked him a lot.

I actually saw him the other night on TV. He's in his 70s now, but he looks good and I'm glad he's still doing what he loves.

It's a good time of year to think of him, then, and to think about second chances. I have no idea whether or not he was remembering the story of the lost dog when he helped me so long ago, but I'd like to think so. I'd like to think he remembered being young and scared and messing up, and getting another opportunity.

I'd also like to think that I'll be willing, should the opportunity arise, to be as generous. I would hope so, because even though it's been almost 30 years now, the memory is fresh: Being 15 years old and making a mistake, and being given a second chance by a good man.

His name was Dick Van Dyke, by the way. Did I mention that?

Happy New Year.

Four Months and 13 Days

I'm thinking of two men. No one in particular, although I suspect they exist somewhere. One is almost 78, the other 75. Both recently celebrated their 50th wedding anniversaries. Both started their careers in the late 1940s, prospered during the Eisenhower 50s, managed to raise teenagers during the turbulent 60s, and retired comfortably in the early 1980s. They both enjoy golf, fishing, and bridge. Both happen to have six grandchildren and eagerly await the next generation. They are in remarkably good health, although both have had prostate surgery. They attend the same church. For all intents and purposes, they are the same man.

Except they're not. The reason they're different is complicated, and dark, and not spoken of for the most part. They're different because in June 1944 one of them was finishing the 11th grade, and the other was facing the hedgerows on the beach in Normandy.

An accident of birth, a difference of three years, and two men, obviously alike, are changed by what happened, or did not, and where they were or weren't. Perspective can be everything.

It's been four months since September 11th. I watched and listened, and I was told we would all be different from now on. We are, I'm sure. No one who saw those pictures can help but be changed. In what way is still a question for me. I wonder about it a lot. I also wonder about those who don't have the luxury of reading and interpreting and discussing those events.

I recently watched "13 Days" on DVD. It's an excellent film. I saw it in the theater but wanted to see it again. It tells the story, of course, of the Cuban Missile Crisis, arguably a pivotal (some would say most) point in human history: For a period of almost two weeks, we came very close to nuclear war. The tension in the country was tremendous. The adults talked about it at the office. The kids talked about it at school.

I listened to the commentary by the director. He was in high school at the time, and he went home and wrote down a story about the day and his thoughts. Thirty-five years later he got to make a film about it. He's a few years older than I am.

I'm a member of the largest demographic group born in the last century. I'm a boomer. Toward the tail end, but still one. The director of "13 Days" is one, too. I know a lot of people his age. We are for the most part in the same general stage of life; our differences (if any) are probably economic and geographic. Yet our memories of October 1962 are so different that we might as well be grandparent and grandchild.

I was four years old. I don't remember details of that time. I remember being scared of the sirens, though. Every Saturday at noon the air raid siren would be tested. It was loud and filled the air; people would stop momentarily on the street. I usually hid until it was over. I had no knowledge of ICBMs and warheads, but I dreamt of large objects flying low overhead.

My slightly older boomer friends and I shared a moment in time and are different because of it, but in different ways. They have a story to tell. I have none, but I still dream of objects in the sky. And I turn off the radio when they test the Emergency Broadcast System because it fills me with irrational dread. I know it's just a test. I know that.

We understand more now about children, about their psychology, about what they see and hear when we think they don't. Children in London who huddled underground during the Blitz had to manage their ghosts by themselves. The kids who saw the planes fly into the World Trade Center, over and over again, will be luckier. We will talk about it, try to assuage their fears and minimize the bad dreams.

I listened to and watched teenagers react to September 11th. Their tranquil, secure world had been interrupted and they'll be different. They'll have stories to tell.

I wonder about the 4-year-olds, though. I wonder what they'll remember. I wonder if forty years from now they'll be walking through city streets and catch sight of a low-flying airliner overhead and flinch a little, maybe feel an involuntary lurch of their stomachs. I wonder if they'll understand why. I imagine they'll tell themselves it's just a plane. Planes fly every day.

Listen to your inner child, they say. I have. My inner child wants the siren to stop. The adult me shudders a bit and goes on. I know a siren is just a siren. I know that.

When All Else Fails

Even after almost 20 years here in the Pacific Northwest, I still slip up occasionally and complain about the rain. Just a little, but people look at me as though I was griping about the 24-hour day or those darn phases of the moon. My Southwestern roots run deep, I guess.

I bought a raincoat when we first moved up here. We only had one car, so I commuted on Metro into downtown Seattle from our apartment at Northgate. I was still a little unsure about when or if an umbrella was appropriate, but I saw a lot of raincoats on the bus.

I liked the look of the it. I felt like Bogart, or Walter Cronkite reporting from Europe in World War II. I'd put it on as I left the house and walk to the bus stop feeling grownup and responsible. Give me your best shot, rain. I'm invincible. I am Raincoat Man.

The only problem was that it smelled funny. It had a distinct odor. It wasn't offensive. It smelled like a raincoat ought to. If you have a raincoat it probably smells like this. It was just that it bothered me. It stirred up dark corners of my mind. It made me think I had wandered into a room I shouldn't have, seen something I wasn't meant to see. I would get slightly nauseated.

I wondered about an allergic reaction, but deep down I knew it was something else. I like to think my life is an open book with no missing moments in my memory, but there was something about a raincoat I really didn't want to remember. Something from a long time ago.

I want to note here that I had a happy childhood. My parents were loving and responsible, and worked hard to give their kids a decent home life. I have no complaints. Still, you hear stories about trauma and abuse, things so overwhelming to a young mind that they become repressed and hidden. I worried.

So I called my mother. We chatted for a while about nothing. I mentioned that I'd bought a raincoat. This got no response, so I told her about the smell and brought up my question of an allergy. She said she thought it was a possibility. I was getting nowhere and starting to envision years of psychotherapy ahead.

I hemmed and hawed, and finally came out with it. Was there some dark secret about a raincoat that I couldn't remember? Something when I was a kid? Mom?

There was silence on the other end. The nausea returned in a big way. My worst suspicions were being confirmed. I waited for what seemed like an eternity. I was beginning to wonder whether the connection had been lost when suddenly I heard what sounded like a gasp, and at that moment I knew. I knew there was silence on the line because my mother was laughing so hard no sound was coming out of her mouth.

It turns out when I was in the first grade, I got a new raincoat. A yellow slicker with clasps in the front. I proudly walked the block to school, went into the classroom...and couldn't undo the clasps. My teacher finally had to help me. I was humiliated. I refused to wear the raincoat again.

I vaguely remember this. Apparently my six-year-old brain decided to spare me the horror of reliving the indignity.

I laugh about it now, but still remember my confusion and the uneasiness of thinking there was something I'd forgotten. I did the right thing, though; I called my mom. Moms always remember.

Mark Twain once remarked that he was amazed that, as he got older, his father seemed to get smarter and smarter. There was a period in my life when I never suspected my parents had any wisdom to share with me. They were useful for money or rides home or a place to live when things went wrong, but I was an adult and knew what was what.

Thank God I'm over that now. I call my parents all the time for advice or help, or just to talk. They seem to have gotten a lot smarter, and sometimes they hold the answers to little mysteries I can't solve on my own.

Every Wednesday morning my mother gets online at her home in Payson, Arizona and reads this column. So thanks, mom, for clearing that raincoat thing up. I can always count on you. And happy birthday, too. Have a great day. Make Dad take you out to dinner. I hope the weather is nice.

It may rain here. I should be used to it after all this time. I still don't own an umbrella. And I threw that raincoat out a long time ago.

By The Content of Their Character

I took a good, hard look at my future around the first of the year, and seeing that it included elastic waistbands and possibly a shot at the leading role in "Orson Welles: The Later Years", I decided to start exercising more.

So almost every day I drag myself out of the house and walk around the neighborhood. I usually pass the fire station. They always seem to be busy in there. I suppose that's normal, although sometimes I wonder if I cause it, if a death row call echoes through the building ("Fat man walking!") and they scurry around to get oxygen and defibrillators just in case.

There are fewer flowers in front of the fire station these days. It was a different story a couple of months ago, when there was an altar of bouquets on the lawn. I guess firefighters have returned to being quiet heroes. For a while there, though, they reminded a nation not just of their everyday sacrifices, but also of how much we missed them. Heroes, I mean.

Somehow we've become a culture of clay feet. The politics of personal destruction and unauthorized biographies have been nudged along by this odd tendency of the subjects themselves to rush to Oprah or Larry or Charlie and fess up. "We're just schmucks like everyone else," they seem to say, unworthy of our adulation. A few years back, NBA star Charles Barkley wagged his finger at America's parents and said, "I'm not a role model."

Okay, you made your point, but gee whiz, Mr. Barkley...doncha wanna be?

Lincoln suffered from depression. Jefferson fathered children out of wedlock with one of his slaves. Washington was superstitious. FDR had a mistress. So did Ike. Kennedy had-- forget it. Lindbergh was an anti-Semite. Mickey Mantle was a drunk. I don't want to even know about Mickey Mouse. Where have you gone, Joe Dimaggio?

A nation yearns for a hero. Someone who simply stood up for what was right, sacrificed personal welfare, loved our country, saw what was possible and dreamed the impossible dream. Isn't there someone out there we can point out to our children without needing to find a flaw somewhere? Someone we can build a monument to, or write a song about, or celebrate with a national holiday?

Wait. Didn't we have Monday off?

It's a curious thing, this Martin Luther King, Jr. Day. It's been around over 15 years and we seem still a little unsure what to do about it. Forget the politicians; they could give you a dozen sound bites based on Groundhog Day. What's the community doing? There seems to be a tendency to make this sort of a Black History or Black Culture day. I suspect Dr. King would be disappointed. Me, too; this has a Brown vs. The Board of Education feel to it. Let's give equal time, but we're still separate.

"An injustice to one threatens justice for all," he said. If some of us are not equal, then none of us are, he thought, and he was jailed, threatened, wiretapped, and attacked because he decided to prove his point. When Rosa Parks refused to give up her seat and Martin Luther King, Jr. was thrust into the public spotlight, the solution to changing an unjust law was obvious to him. The African-American community in Montgomery, Alabama may have been second-class citizens, but they made up a majority of the bus riders in that city. Under Dr. King's leadership, they didn't fire bomb the bus headquarters or burn the buses or file massive class action lawsuits. They just walked. Instead of riding segregated buses, they walked for over a year until they achieved their goal.

He sought his strength and his methods from his faith, and the Gospels. "Do to us what you will," he wrote, "and we will still love you. But we will wear you down by our capacity to suffer." In a time when prominent Christian leaders are seen on television pleading for money to support their networks or lambasting those who don't agree with them, it seems remarkable that this Baptist minister simply loved his enemies and changed them, and us, as a result.

He lived every day knowing he was in the sniper's scope, and one day he was. He was 39. He wanted a long life, but he had lived long enough to get to the mountaintop. And in doing so, he showed us what heroism is all about.

Oh, America, you have a hero. You have lots of them. I pass them every day at the fire station. They come in all sizes and all colors. They put country above home and community above self. They can't be threatened or frightened away from their causes. They believe that service to others is their highest calling. They all cherish their children's futures. And they all dream.

If I Had A Hammer

My daughter's car wouldn't start the other day, and it took me four days to get around to figuring out what was wrong and fixing it.

It's not really her car, of course. It's my car in every technical, legal and moral sense, but then so is my phone and I haven't been able to use that in years.

Four days is actually sort of a speed record in my car repair history. When I was young and foolish, I once decided to put a new transmission in my '69 Mustang by myself and it took me just under three months. You think I'm joking.

This problem came shortly after a very large car repair bill, so I was relieved when it turned out just to be a bad solenoid. This is worth mentioning for two reasons: (1) It's a cheap and easy fix, twenty bucks and a couple of bolts, and (2) I actually repaired something.

It's not that I'm incompetent generally. I can solve computer problems, set up home electronic equipment, roast a chicken, read music, program a VCR, change a diaper, bake bread, mow the lawn, operate a washing machine, feed the dog, and understand some Spanish. All of which makes me well rounded in my world. Unfortunately, my world doesn't appear to be the real world. Or else I fell asleep in high school when they were teaching the course How Most Things Work.

It's not that I don't try. It's my theory that I simply lack a couple of genes; specifically, those that are responsible for reading instructions and measuring. Give me a section of wall with an electrical outlet, for example, and tell me to panel it. I will carefully measure the distance from ceiling to floor, side to side, and when I'm done I will have a paneled wall with a cut-out for an outlet that is usually several feet away, and sometimes in another room.

I was able to compensate for this fairly well until a couple of years ago, when my brother-in-law moved away. My brother-in-law, whose name is Jim Welch, was transferred from Washington to California, where he's a vice-president for a large company. I'm not really sure what he does for them, but I assume on his lunch breaks he re-wires the building or shores up the foundation or something. As far as I'm concerned, he's a combination of Thomas Edison and that guy on PBS who makes furniture from, like, pieces of wood and stuff.

One day I came home from work and found Jim in my kitchen, installing our dishwasher. When we bought a new front door, Jim just happened to drop by to see how things were going, which was fortunate considering I was at that moment putting up a sign reading "Please Don't Rob Us" across this gaping hole in my house. We bought a home with an unfinished basement (yes, what a good idea), and when 12 years ago I decided to turn part of it into a home office Jim came over and graciously framed it and put up drywall. He then carefully showed me how to finish the taping and sanding. Which I truly intend to do.

My father, too, is a "can fix anything" guy. When I was growing up, he was constantly remodeling our house, installing new plumbing, laying brick walkways, and telling me to please get out of his way before I hurt myself or he was forced to do it for me. I've found myself painting a room, simultaneously wondering whether I should have put a drop cloth on the carpeting and if a convenience store was the best place to buy paint, when I imagine him standing over my shoulder, cigarette dangling from his lips, rolling his eyes.

I think of Jackie Gleason in the movie "Smokey And The Bandit", when he turns to his hapless son and says something like, "I refuse to believe you sprang from my loins." I think my dad feels the same way sometimes, although Mom probably has an opinion about that.

The more I think about it, it may be just me. I seem to recall all of my neighbors at different times doing handy things with screwdrivers. My wife repairs the garbage disposal or toilet when we have problems. My son can spend hours putting things together and taking them apart, carefully reading the instructions. I assume if my daughter cared about such matters she'd be competent, too.

I can replace a solenoid, though, and that's enough for me. Or should be, except that I've been worrying about my front deck for the last couple of years. It looks sort of rickety and unsafe. I guess I'll just have to take care of it myself.

I'm thinking of painting it.

Home Alone

When I was in elementary school, I saw an article about the history of the telephone. It showed pictures of the early phones and how they had changed over the years, and, at the end, an artist's conception of a videophone, which according to the article was expected to become commonplace sometime in the near future. Probably around 1970.

So I take predictions with a grain of salt. It's 2002 and we still don't have utopia, flying cars, or videophones, but we also haven't had a nuclear war or President Gingrich, so I guess we're doing okay.

A few years ago, a nation of telecommuters was the current prediction. We'd all work from home and drive-time traffic jams would be relics of the past, they said. According to a recent survey of businesses, it hasn't happened yet. There are more people telecommuting, but usually only once or twice a week. I have somewhat of a jaded opinion about this, having worked at home for the past 13 years. If this eventually becomes the norm, I've got news for the rest of you. I have seen the future, and it's weird.

When I started, I had a lot of fun calculating not just the time I gained that I wasn't spending sitting in traffic, but also the savings from gas and wear and tear on the car. What I didn't count on was the sock budget. If you're like me and you work at home, you don't wear shoes a lot, which means you pad around in stocking feet all day long. Socks weren't meant for this kind of abuse; I was soon walking around the house with flapping bits of material wrapped around my feet like someone out of Dickens.

Then there were just the human maintenance issues. There's no need to jump out of bed and into the shower if you're just going down to the basement to work. Shaving becomes an afterthought, deodorant for a special occasion only. I tended to eat, sleep, and work in the same clothes, sometimes for weeks at a time. At the end of my first year, I had a bushy beard and a ponytail, no socks, and I really didn't smell all that good.

I turned from a white guy to a Person Of No Color. My blondish hair became dirty brown. I went from 160 pounds soaking wet to 240 and upward. My social skills disappeared; I got nervous talking to people on the phone and shrank into a corner at parties. I never saw people I worked with. A strange woman once appeared at my door and handed me a Christmas present, and it was only after she left that I realized she must have been the person who had been signing my paychecks for the past year.

Scientific studies have shown that if you separate a rat from the others, put it in a room with little light for 12 hours a day, give it no exercise and a lot of fatty foods, at the end of a year it will stagger out, obese and sluggish, adverse to sunlight and social interaction, looking like a Marlon Brando rat, with an addiction to chat rooms and Oprah. This was me.

One day I was refilling ice trays for the freezer, taking pride in the fact that even without an icemaker I had ensured there were plenty of ice cubes in the bin, when I suddenly had an epiphany.

We all have these moments of clarity, when our lives suddenly become clear and distinct and we see who we are and what we do. I had suddenly realized that making ice had become my hobby.

So I changed. I became active in church. My wife had gone back to school so I started cooking. Every day I would go to the grocery store, spotting bargains and practicing talking with the checkout people. I can't imagine leaving the house to work in an office somewhere, but after 13 years I've managed to sort of rejoin the human race. It seems about the same. I haven't seen any flying cars yet.

There are benefits to working at home, no question. I've always been there when my kids come home from school. I've learned how to marinate and how to bake bread. I can always be reached by phone. I've become friends with UPS drivers and neighbors and grocery store workers.

We're social animals, though, and if the future holds a nation of telecommuters I have some advice. Walk a lot. Get out of the house and talk to people. Take a shower every day. Don't worry so much about the ice cubes.

And invest in socks. Trust me on this. There's a future in socks.

The Little Church That Could

When Thomas Jefferson sent Lewis and Clark down the Missouri to explore our neck of the woods, he mused that perhaps they'd find the Lost Tribes of Israel. Who knew? In a young country whose frontiers had just begun to be broached, we might as well have been at the end of the earth.

A church that has served Mukilteo since 1907 is worth remarking on, then. That's a long time in Northwest years.

Mark Smith is the pastor of Mukilteo Presbyterian Church and knows its history well. He has to; some members of his congregation have been attending MPC for the better part of its 95 years.

Continuity is strong here. A photo from the 1950s shows a smiling little girl, standing on the church steps; she's now an elder and was on the search committee that recommended Mark for his job.

The Pacific Northwest is the most unchurched area in the country, for unclear reasons. Maybe it's a remnant of our frontier psyche, telling us there are more important things to do than sit in a pew and listen to a sermon. Maybe it's just that Sunday is a nice day to ski.

It makes it a sellers market for mission work, though, and Mark Smith laughs as he points at this quiet, residential block of Third Street where MPC sits. "On any given day, maybe four or five cars come down this street," he says. It's hard to serve your neighbors when they can't see you.

So with all the hullabaloo about the fate of Rosehill, it might surprise you to learn that the oldest church in town, housed in one of the oldest buildings, will be gone soon.

Well, not gone, exactly. The Lord moves in mysterious ways, and sometimes the operative word is "move." Mukilteo Presbyterian hopes to break ground on the Nelson farm this April, and God willing (of course) by the end of the year a multi-purpose structure will stand (Phase I of their goals), ready to serve a much larger population than in 1907.

While visibility is the main reason behind the move, space is the final frontier for the folks at MPC. Mark's office has a glorious view of the Sound and the square footage of a decent bathroom. It's so small the mice are hunchbacked. He has to step outside to change his mind. Stop me now.

He talks of squeezing 20 teenagers like a '50s fraternity prank into a Sunday School room the size of a closet. A congregation of over 350 worships and studies in a facility adequate for maybe a third of that. Situated on a corner, surrounded by houses, there's no room to expand and even less to park.

The church building will have to be sold before they make their move, and what will happen to it is a concern for many in Mukilteo. We have problems letting go of these old buildings.

They hold our ghosts; we can run our fingers along the walls and stir up voices from decades ago. We grieve about time, even though we know it's a losing battle. Things change.

What will happen to MPC is that they'll continue doing what they have for almost a century, just down the road a bit.

A major part of Phase II will be constructing a new, larger home for Mukilteo Food Bank. Phase III will involve a sanctuary with a greater capacity. Mark Smith envisions concerts, youth activities, possibly a preschool; and there will still be the AA meetings and Boy Scout gatherings, etc., all the quiet things a community church does so well.

The irony has always been that for those who have no interest in church, they will attend only at the most significant moments of their lives. Many of you will take little note of MPC's move, but you'll see your children married and mourn your loved ones in their sanctuary.

A year from now, the faithful will gather at the new Mukilteo Presbyterian Church on a Sunday morning and worship as they always have. They'll pass the plate and sing the doxology. They'll break bread and sip grape juice (they're Presbyterians).

Perhaps Mark Smith will hold an infant, sprinkle her head with water, proclaim her a child of God and a ward of the congregation. He'll walk down the aisles with her, holding her up for all to see.

She'll have no idea, of course, of the effort involved in building the first church in 1907, or the next in 2002. The past is meaningless to her at this moment; she is a creature of the future.

She is, in fact, asleep in her pastor's arms, loved and blessed, unaware that she has been bound in baptism to generations that went before, and those yet to come. She just knows she's in good hands, and she is.

March Madness

Winter went out like a lamb, I guess, if you count the snow we had last week as the final gasp. Compared to the accumulation at my house in late January, this was nothing, a dusting, maybe an inch.

Snow in Western Washington is a sociable thing. It brings us out of the house to get reacquainted with our neighbors, and everybody laughs and we shake our heads and swear we've never seen anything like it, when of course we have.

And there's always some guy stuck in the snow, spinning his wheels on the side of the road, and when you ask if you can help he smiles grimly and shakes his head and says, "I used to live in Montana."

To a lot of people, this would be an odd non sequitor, sort of like asking someone how their mom is doing and having them answer that their favorite food is lasagna, but we understand. Snow lets otherwise uninteresting people feel smug and arrogant, so they can complain that no one up here knows how to drive in the snow and how we all panic, etc. People like this is why God created ditches, if you ask me.

The snow is gone now, though, and spring is right around the corner and I'm dreading it. Winter covers a lot of indiscretions, but spring tends to snap the blanket off and tell us to get up and start moving. The grass is going to start growing and the gutters are clogged and the garage needs cleaning and there's a Christmas tree in the dining room.

What, you ask, is a Christmas tree doing in my dining room in the middle of March? Simple: I got tired of it being in the living room.

My wife does the tree every year. Since she gave up fighting her allergies every Christmas and we switched to an artificial one, I'm not needed for lifting and other manly acts and that's fine with me. I don't know where she stores all the ornaments and lights and things; all I know is one day in mid-December we have a decorated tree in the living room.

This year, for some reason, she decided she didn't have time to take it down so it just stayed there, past the Twelve Days of Christmas, past January, past Groundhog Day, past Valentine's Day, and one day in late February I got energized by self-righteousness and embarrassment and dragged it into the dining room, and that's where it is.

To be fair, I should note that my wife is in her last year of graduate school and is either in class, interning at a hospital, or studying and writing papers. Her time is extremely limited, and she has priorities that don't include taking down the tree.

But there's a Christmas tree in the dining room. I mean, come on. There's a point where you go past lovable eccentricity and just become weird. Our household has become the equivalent of Michael Jackson.

It's not that I'm dysfunctional when it comes to straightening up. I just don't know where the ornaments go and my tendency would be to throw them all in a paper sack and probably break half of them, so I do nothing and every day I walk by a

Christmas tree in my dining room and wonder how my life turned out the way it has.

If you're thinking this sounds like an episode of "The Simpsons" that's exactly what I'm thinking. Not that we've ever been your normal, wash-the-dishes-after-dinner sort of family. My kids learned to walk by negotiating around stacks of books and piles of laundry and once for almost a year an old water heater.

I blame this on my wife, which sounds sort of mean except her mother blames it on her, too. My mother-in-law actually apologized to me once for not teaching her daughter how to be neat, but I think it's more of a philosophical condition than bad habits. My wife is an extremely intelligent, efficient, and energetic person. She just believes in the Cleaning Fairy.

For example, when we're due to have company, my first move is to make a list of things that need to be cleaned, sterilized or thrown away. My wife's reaction is to do laundry and/or buy a new car.

So she has no problem with a Christmas tree in the dining room, and apparently neither do my kids, so I guess I should just get over it. I have other things to think about, anyway. The lawn mower needs a tune-up. The garage is going to take a whole weekend. And I still have to take down the Halloween decorations.

On second thought, maybe not. October will be here before we know it.

Justice For All

I got out of the habit of watching TV regularly a few years ago, but one day last week I woke up with a temperature of 103 and handling a remote control was the extent of my abilities, so I got reacquainted.

Newt Minow called it a vast wasteland forty years ago and it seems to have gotten vaster but not better. Sixty channels, half of which are devoted to selling either exercise equipment, food processors, or religion. Of the rest, about ten show mediocre movies, five are variations of ESPN, and about five, as far as I can tell, run only episodes of "Matlock." This leaves weather, news, and cooking.

I like cooking shows, actually. The joy of preparing good food leaps off the screen, and given my fever and tendency to fade into unconsciousness, and one show after another, I had the fascinating experience of seeing a chef shove Irish soda bread into the oven and in the blink of an eye take out Peking duck. It was magic.

In the early afternoon I switched to CNN and caught breaking news. The jury in the Andrea Yates case had returned a verdict after less than four hours of deliberation. Guilty of murder.

I was lucid enough by then to be reasonable, and I dug deeply into my left-leaning, bleeding-heart, NPR-listening soul and decided it was OK with me.

I know she's sick. Schizophrenia is a horrible disease; living life with imaginary voices and images is its own kind of hell, I would think. Toss in some twisted theology and we begin to glimpse how this horrible act happened.

But she killed her kids. With premeditation she took each of her five children, from six months to seven years of age, and held them underwater until they drowned. I can accept the idea that in her psychotic state she imagined she was saving their souls from Satan, but she knew it was illegal and called the cops. Case closed, at least in Texas.

I had no wish for Andrea Yates to be put to death. It would have soothed no one, deterred no one, and made no one feel safer. And if she had been found innocent by reason of insanity and sent to a mental institution, I would have slept no less soundly. I could imagine, though, after a year or so, her being announced cured or at least manageable and released.

Maybe it's a parental chauvinism; we've accepted and dealt with this enormous responsibility of caring for little human beings and perhaps we look more harshly on those who breach that trust. She forced her 7-year-old son underwater while he screamed, "I'm sorry!" for whatever offense he might have committed, and the idea that she could be allowed to resume life as usual just seems wrong.

The camera wandered to Russell Yates. He had stuck by his wife's defense, wanting an innocent result. He was the picture of compassion. I wondered about him.

I used to work mostly with women, and occasionally I'd encounter a husband who was odd, who made conversation with me in a phony, cheerful way, who seemed to be checking me out for designs on his wife. It doesn't take a psychology degree to recognize insecurity and someone who controls his spouse to what most of us would think is an excessive degree. I tried to be polite and mention my wife in every other sentence.

So I wonder about Russell Yates. I wonder why he let his wife live with five children in a bus. I wonder why he wasn't more concerned about two suicide attempts and instead encouraged her to have another child. I wonder about the lack of self esteem Andrea Yates had and the crushing responsibility of home schooling five kids. I wonder what he was thinking.

He's lost his entire family, of course, and sympathy is the natural inclination. Maybe it was the fever, but I looked at him and I thought, what did you do?, and then realized that was the wrong question.

This time of year, Christians mark The Passion of Jesus, and Pontius Pilate is remembered. He washed his hands in public, abdicating his responsibility.

Society could not prevent five children from being murdered by their mother. Maybe nobody could have, but I have questions about this man who apparently controlled his wife's life so completely. The lesson of Pilate is that the responsibility for an atrocity is borne not only by those who commit it, but by those who have the power to stop it and do nothing.

I turned off the TV. My kids came home then, and fussed about me and felt my forehead and wondered who would make dinner. I felt better. At least you can live with the flu.

The Inside-Out Boy

When my son John was 4 years old, we sat outside on a summer night and stared at the stars, and he told me of another lifetime.

"I was a man once," he said matter-of-factly, "and I drove a red car. It crashed in the desert and I died and went to heaven. I liked it there but God said you needed me here, so I came." Years later he claimed not to remember this, or speculated that he got the idea from TV. I wonder.

As a baby, he wouldn't meet your eye. He'd play for hours by himself with a single toy, all the time humming or babbling. He could be impulsive to an alarming degree, fixating on one object or goal with enormous concentration. He loved to laugh and had a great one, loud and hooting. It took him longer than usual to begin to talk.

He was extremely sensitive to smells and tastes, and the way clothes felt on his body. He'd wear his shirts and sweat pants inside out to avoid the feel of the tags on his skin. One day he came into the kitchen dressed in his usual layers of clothing, all backwards, and his sister laughed. "Here comes the inside-out boy," she said.

My son is autistic. He has Asperger's Syndrome (AS), a neurological condition, a wiring thing. People with AS lack the ability to perceive nonverbal clues, to read body language and understand inflection and intonation, things most of us learn innately at a young age. Social norms are often bewildering to them. Innocent comments or loud voices can be interpreted as threats. They sometimes stand too close, say inappropriate things, and get frustrated by messages they can't receive.

They can share traits with sufferers of more severe, debilitating forms of autism: Certain repetitive movements, tics and twitches, vocal mannerisms and odd speech. AS people are fortunate, though, in that they often desire to reach out from inside their isolated shells to interact with the rest of us; they just don't know how.

It's a hopeful condition. Many Asperger's people are very productive and special members of society, and they were long before autism was identified. We can look back through history at inventors, writers, artists of all sorts and speculate. The title character in neurologist Oliver Sacks' book "The Anthropologist From Mars" is a good example of a very functional person who has Asperger's Syndrome.

I'm writing about this because John asked me to. He thinks it would be helpful if more people understood this condition, and particularly if more of us understood that people who are different can also be interesting.

He goes to a special school where a good deal of time is spent on social interaction. John sometimes creates a script for himself when he's about to enter a stressful situation. He practices comments and behaviors. He works harder at ordinary life than most of us ever will.

There's a tendency currently for some media pundits to disparage the idea that a child not in a wheelchair or undergoing chemotherapy might have unseen problems. They fret sarcastically that we've become a nation of syndromes, of acronyms and over-diagnosis. They imagine doctors standing by with bottles and needles, ready to medicate at the slightest hint of originality or creativity.

They don't talk to parents and teachers, of course. They don't talk to me, which is probably a good idea as there are certain times I don't suffer fools very well.

I've learned a lot in 12 years. I've learned how to wander through the maze of support services. I've learned how to imagine life through the eyes of a stranger in a strange land. I've learned to admire teachers like Ann King and physicians like Cheryl Beighle, who saw not a problem but a little boy.

I've learned that character often is not forged by how we endure adversity, but how we approach it. John worries about the future, but he'd never say he was afflicted. He thinks he's been blessed with a special gift to see the world in a different way, thereby effectively taking the "dis" out of disability.

He sometimes sees himself as Data, the android from "Star Trek" who yearned to become human. I understand this, but there are times, when he senses I'm having a rough day and hugs me, ruffles my hair and tells me I'm a great dad, that I think he's the most human person I know.

I don't know what he thinks of my life, but I know he loves me. I don't know what his future holds, but I'm confident it's bright. I don't know if he was sent here from heaven by God because I needed him. I have no idea.

I think about it a lot, though.

Over The Rainbow

I was going to write about something completely different this week, but then I had sort of a vision. You have to take visions seriously.

For various reasons, I was inching along in traffic Saturday morning in the Northgate area, a neighborhood I lived in when I was in my 20s and broke and wondering what the future held. I was feeling nostalgic, and then I saw her.

It startled me; for a moment I thought I knew her. She was young, about 25 or so, walking briskly down the sidewalk, head held high. She had dark brown hair and was very pretty, and she was looking straight ahead, smiling, as if good things were waiting for her somewhere. Seeing her, I suddenly stumbled back 20 years.

I was 23, and I'd been hired as a cast member in a dinner theater in northern Arizona. I got the job mostly because they needed a baritone and I could write skits for the show; it wasn't my dancing, trust me. I arrived for our first musical rehearsal and was sitting at a table, waiting for my turn, when she walked in the door.

I thought I recognized her at first, that I knew her somehow. She had dark brown hair and was very pretty, and she swept into the room with a smile.

I managed to work my way through my song, and as I sat back down she leaned over to me and said, "Y'all have a nice voice," her Texas diphthongs ringing in my ears. Then she went up to the stage and sat down on the stool by the piano, and she sang.

I don't remember the song, but I like to think it was "Somewhere Over The Rainbow", which is my favorite of her repertoire. Probably not, but she smiled at me and she sang like an angel.

Being the newest members of the cast and so the lowest on the totem pole, the two of us were given the job of vacuuming the carpet before the theater opened that night. It wasn't hard work, and at some point I chivalrously offered to finish the job alone. She laughed. "That's all right, I do a lot of vacuuming."

I note that this is the only time she ever told me an outright lie, by the way.

Listen, young people: This is how life happens. One day you vacuum the floor together, a year later you drive up to a ridge overlooking the red rocks of Sedona, and surrounded by friends and family you get married. Two months later you put all your belongings into a small trailer and move to Seattle, hope in your hearts and $500 in your pockets and everything ahead of you.

I watched as she grew, as she moved her way from Seattle Opera Chorus member and small parts in musicals to leading roles in operas, concerts, and recitals. She became a familiar face and voice in the music scene in Western Washington and British Columbia.

There were also babies and mortgages and arguments and stuff, but mostly I watched my wife sing and make people happy.

A world-class singer who is semi-retired and now lives in this area told me once that he considered Julie Kae one of the top three sopranos in the world. He seemed a little bewildered that this was such a secret, but my wife's goals were never about fame and fortune.

Four years ago she had a calling to serve in another way, and this June she finishes seminary. Last week we got the news that she passed her ordination exams, the big hurdle, which with her degree now will allow her to be called as a pastor of a church.

I know her secrets. I know her history and her strengths; I know her flaws and failings. I've watched her for twenty years and sometimes I've wondered why, but never for very long.

I tried to explain to my daughter the other night that, in my feeble father's philosophy, life is like a movie. In the technical sense, I mean: A series of moments, discrete and isolated, which with the persistence of vision and the arbitrary measure of years give the illusion of motion. The moments are still there, though, which is why her grandmothers could easily tell her what it's like to be 17. They are still 17.

So am I, for that matter. I'm still 17, and 30, and 43, all at once. I'm still 23, and I sit in an empty theater and listen. I'm young and callow, but I know that the future is a mystery and that happiness is fleeting and should be embraced; and at that moment I feel I would be content to sit there and listen to her sing forever.

The Lion, The Witch, and The Other Witch

"Brigadoon" is the story of a village in a state of perpetual adolescence; aging one day per century, it's in the world but not of it.

It's an appealing story. Statements about earning our gray hairs aside, we all grow up because we have no choice in the matter; we can't really know if we would have been content to be, say, 16 forever.

I saw "Brigadoon" Friday night at Kamiak High, watching the third generation of high school thespians in my family (I'm not counting my wife; sometimes we don't count her).

I watched the cast members celebrate, and if I'd been stupid enough to mention to them that I knew how they felt, I would have gotten one of those looks they reserve for that sort of thing.

I was in six musicals in high school, an age when theater is all about passion and fearing failure and getting up there anyway, about friends and feelings and dark corners backstage where romance gets a chance and things can get lively. There are lots of stories to tell.

When I was 16, I played the Tin Man in "The Wizard Of Oz." It wasn't our best show, but it was memorable for two reasons: A little incident in a parking lot, and the fact that our Wicked Witch was played by a boy.

Emil Miller was one of the guys for whom words fall short and you really had to know him, but he was interesting. He was a professional musician while still a teenager, he carried a briefcase and wore a coat and tie, and he could talk a school administrator out of his petty cash and get a thank you note in return. Emil had a long history and the rest of us looked at him with more than a little awe.

Casting Emil as the witch was actually an easy call; behind make-up and costume his gender was impossible to know, and he had a great witch voice.

Because this was a children's show, we got to do a little publicity tour of the elementary and middle schools in our district, drumming up business. We drove around all day in full costume and makeup, giving previews and distracting drivers.

We had just finished at the junior high that most of us had attended when one of our drivers backed into another in the parking lot. It was just a fender bender, nobody got hurt, but Ms. Bailey, the girl's gym teacher, came out to investigate.

Ms. Bailey we remembered. She'd been mean and nasty in our day and still was, and she marched up to us and began making snide comments about teenagers racing around small parking lots.

This went on for a few minutes, and then Emil had enough and calmly suggested to Ms. Bailey that perhaps she would be more comfortable if she simply returned to the rock she had apparently crawled out from under.

Things got interesting. Mr. Gomeric, the longtime principal, came roaring out of his office, preparing to have a few teenagers for lunch. To his credit, the sight of a cowardly lion, scarecrow, tin man, and wicked witch in his parking lot didn't even slow him up.

"So what's this about the Tin Man making a comment to Miss Bailey?" he barked out with, amazingly, a straight face.

I had an ethical dilemma, then, hard enough for any teenager and not helped by the fact that shaking uncontrollably in a sheet metal costume is a noisy business, but Emil saved me. "I said it, Mr. Gomeric."

A male voice coming from a wicked witch has an effect not unlike ventriloquism, apparently, and Mr. Gomeric looked confused. Emil took a couple of steps in his direction, using his broom to make points. "He didn't say it, I did." The principal still seemed a little puzzled, so he added, "It's me, Mr. Gomeric. It's Emil."

As I said, Emil had a long history. Mr. Gomeric got this little smile on his face, almost wistful, and he said, "Ah. Emil. " And that was that. End of story.

I saw Emil Miller last summer in Phoenix, where he owns a recording studio. We reminisced, but somehow we didn't get around to the story of the two witches in the parking lot. It was probably just as well; it's awkward for middle-aged men to recall that some of their happiest moments were spent wearing makeup and tights.

I wouldn't blame a "Brigadoon" cast member for doubting that this old fat guy could understand how he feels, but I do. You forget a lot of things, more than you're comfortable with, but you never forget standing backstage when you're 16, waiting to go on.

It will be over so soon, I want to tell them, savor the moment and seize the day, but they wouldn't listen and neither would I. The rest of the world moves on, I thought then, but I will always be here, waiting in the wings for the overture to start.

Memories Of The Monte Vista Hotel

It's a particular conceit of mine that I don't have stereotypical male behaviors. I don't ogle women. I essentially couldn't care less about cars as long as they run. I can put a new roll of toilet paper in the holder. I'm not afraid to cry at sad movies or use coupons. I cook, sweep, shop, mop, and help with homework. I am, then, like Mary Poppins, practically perfect in every way.

Except I won't ask for help. I won't ask where the soy sauce is in the grocery store, I won't ask how to spell a word, I won't ask for advice, and the day I ask for directions is the day you put me in a dress and call me girly boy. I have my limits.

I was in trouble last week, though. I had a broken lawnmower and knee-high grass and weeds with an attitude. Procrastination had led me to a sunny Saturday with work to do and no tools. I needed help and so called my friend Paul, and I was happy to have a reason.

I met Paul Morin in the summer of 1980, when we were doing repertory theater in northern Arizona. Looking back, it seems now we spent less time interpreting Sam Shepherd and Noel Coward and more doing manual labor, and cleaning out a prop room late one night Paul and I started talking and we've never stopped.

I don't know how it works. Love gets defined by music and poetry, but friendship has a thousand beginnings and it's hard to find a constant. You grow up together, you work together, you share interests: Lots of reasons to be friends, but sometimes something just clicks.

We completed each other's sentences and made each other laugh. We shared a mutual fear-and-fascination appreciation of our leading lady, an Oscar-winning actress who was past her prime but could still intimidate with the best of them. She was Irish and loud, and she hated the fact that she was stuck in the boonies with kids doing basically theater for tourists.

"Marx Brothers material!" was one of her favorite comments about our lack of professionalism, along with "This is amateur night in Dixie!" These became mantras for us, Paul and I, as we spent hours after rehearsal in the Monte Vista Hotel bar, alienating the rest of the crew as our two-person monologue jumped from subject to subject.

"This is Marx Brothers material!" we'd yell, ordering another pitcher of beer and lining up Billy Joel on the jukebox. We entertained and inspired each other, and that one summer we were inseparable.

He married his college sweetheart and I married mine. We landed in the Pacific Northwest, both of us dreaming of maybe starting a theater company or writing a play about a fading actress called "Amateur Night In Dixie", and eventually learning that responsibility, like grass, grows regardless of your inattention. Real jobs and families happened along the way, and now thirty minutes apart with 20-plus years of friendship and I hadn't seen him in almost two years.

He brought his mower and weed trimmer and leaf blower and we did the job; three hours on a Saturday we both had found free, surprisingly, him with three boys on different baseball teams and me with work piling up.

We loaded the equipment back in his Suburban and stood in the sun and laughed at the gray in each other's hair. We griped that we hadn't had enough time to talk, how we didn't do this nearly often enough and needed to, the things we always say.

"How many springs and summers do we have left?" he asked suddenly, and I realized then that there is a poetry of friendship after all; it speaks of regret and laments time slipping through our fingers, and I resolved to work harder.

Maybe I'll ask him to help me with my deck or the blackberry bushes, or maybe we'll just find a bar like the Monte Vista that has pitchers of beer and Billy Joel on the jukebox.

"You may be right/I may be crazy" he sings, and the waitress will wonder what these two guys could be talking about so fast and so loud. Hours will pass and our cell phones will ring, our wives asking what we're doing when they really know, they must, after all these years.

This is Marx Brothers material, we think, life pulling us in so many directions when all we want is time to talk. We shake our heads and laugh and go home to our lawns and our kids, knowing our days and hours are numbered now but cherishing the company just the same as we always did, back when we had nothing but time.

Men Don't Leave

My wife refused to marry me until I was 25. She's slightly older and had a thing about it.

(Did I say slightly? I meant barely, a trivial amount, almost negligible.)

This was the only requirement, and it was easy; it wasn't like I had to have, you know, a job or something.

Twenty-five is a good age to get married, I think, especially if you're planning a family. Young enough to still have some energy, but old enough to have learned some patience and developed enough fortitude to change a diaper without throwing up.

I was thinking about the missing men, here with Father's Day coming up. The ones who leave, who abandon their families. I wonder how many got married too young.

I can imagine him, 18 and in love, and he gets married and life happens and suddenly he's 24 with three kids and no money. Maybe he's a good man, works hard and tries to do his best, but it's a petrifying responsibility and one day he just runs.

Birthday cards and money from a distance are nice but not enough, not nearly enough, and even if his kids get curious when they're older and find some sort of reconciliation, there's a hole that can't be filled in retrospect. There are things you're supposed to learn from your father.

It's a sad story, suitable for a cable movie or a thin novel with a title like, "A Second Summer" or "A Time To Heal." Maybe the father is dying; that's always a nice touch. It's a good story, a real tearjerker, and it always begs a question for me:

What if he doesn't?

Is it still a good story if he doesn't leave? The fear stays too, it's always there, and he gets up early in the morning and drinks his coffee and shakes, wondering how he can possibly do this. He has a decent job, but he can't see how there will ever be enough money. He gets dressed, though, and goes to work every day just the same.

He's 34 before he can buy a house. Years of renting, moving from neighborhood to neighborhood, job to better job, but he does, finally. The kids are teenagers now, and they're irritating and perplexing but they do well in school and there are no problems with drugs or jail or pregnancies.

Some of their friends, the boys, seem drawn to him and seek him out. Maybe he wonders about this, wonders what they want. He doesn't see it but there's something substantial about him, something solid and serious, and teenage boys can't express it but they recognize it as a good thing to be, something men should be.

College comes and there's no money, it's been spent on surviving, but his kids are good students and they get scholarships and jobs and it works out fine, and suddenly he's 40-ish and freer. There are always midlife demons to chase, though, and life doesn't get any easier.

He still goes to work every day, and on weekends he makes a list of projects and chores to do, crossing them off as he finishes. His family teases him about his slow ways, his meticulous and careful construction, with the deck or the workbench or the patio or the plumbing. He's slow, he is, but the craftsman is hardwired in his soul and what he makes doesn't break, and it lasts.

He harbors regrets, and when he speaks of his kids he's proud but points to his wife and says it was her, she did it all by herself, not me. His children know better.

The younger son calls him one night, deep in his cups and his own midlife demon chase, and he asks him then: "Did you ever think about leaving?"

He's 65 but he remembers, he still shudders when he sees a junky car with diaper bags in the backseat, and he gives his son no advice, no admonitions, no words of wisdom, just the truth. "Oh yes. Lots of times. Lots of times."

We grieve, we parents, over mistakes and missed opportunities, over dark thoughts and choices we might have made but didn't, and all the time we were there every day, fumbling through the process and going to work, and in watching us our children learned their lessons.

And this is what I learned from my father: Life is difficult. There's always work to be done. Men don't leave.

Two teenagers got married in 1955, and it turned out to be a good story after all. Building a family is hard work, no matter when you start, but done slowly and carefully it won't break, and it lasts. This is simple but it's true, and I know because I learned it from my father.

A Beautiful Day In The Neighborhood

To people from the Southwest, from Arizona or New Mexico or Texas, the Pacific Northwest is what New York City is to a young actor or musician. You either make it or you go home, tail between your legs but grateful to be back among the living. It's not the rain, we tell them, it's the grayness of it all, but you have to live it to know it and then sometimes it's too late to do anything but commit suicide or pack.

I survived my first winter up here, 19 years ago, an Arizona émigré, partly because I had a sneaking suspicion I was being punished for the audacity of leaving home without much of a plan, but mostly because of the preposterousness of it all. The sun has got to come out one of these days, I thought, and sure enough it did and I learned the secret of living up here. I'm not telling, either.

I dream of days like this in December. It's 75 and the sun is seeping through the blinds in my office, whispering that the beach is five minutes away and work can wait. There are other things on my mind, too. My former home state is burning. Edgar Martinez is back in the lineup. Rosemary Clooney and Ann Landers are dead. And they're digging a big hole next door.

The hole used to be the Hunter house. It's gone now and it needed to be, but still. Russell and Judy Hunter were here when we moved in, 14 years ago, and had been for a couple of decades. Their children had played in the woods that became my property.

They were nice people who babysat for us and bought anything my daughter was selling door to door. We always knew when Russ got home from work because a minute later we'd hear Judy start to laugh from inside the house. This is the best kind of voyeurism, hearing joy from your neighbors. They were good ones.

They bulldozed the house and most of the yard, but left the big oak tree down in front. I'm glad; many dark nights I've used that as a landmark for my driveway. And not just me. When my mother-in-law drove the car home from Northwest Hospital with my 5-year-old daughter, leaving my wife and me in the labor room awaiting our impending son, Beth directed her. "Turn at the scary tree," she said, and I've done that a lot.

I did that once many years ago when I needed to for the wrong reasons. I'd gone to see a movie in Seattle with a friend, and we stopped in a bar for a drink before the film started. A discussion ensued and suddenly we'd missed the beginning, so we stayed and drank some more. Eventually my buddy went home to sleep and I stared at my car and the 25 miles of highway waiting for me and I wondered.

It's not something I'm proud of. My height and weight and number of drinks probably would have ensured a legal blood level, but my reflexes were not in the best shape and strangers on the road that night were less safe than they should have been.

I've never done it again, by the way, never gotten behind the wheel under the influence, because that was a scary night and when I saw that oak tree I knew I'd escaped without hurting myself or anyone else, and once was enough. Maybe you only get lucky once.

And sometimes not even then. In the spring of 1995, an off-duty police officer with personal problems and a history of alcohol abuse entered the express lanes on I-5 the wrong way, bursting through the barriers and weaving at high speed until she struck a pick-up truck. You may recall this. I do, because the people she hit were my neighbors.

Russell and Judy Hunter were driving home from visiting family. Russ tried to pull over to the side but there was no room. He suffered multiple fractures, but Judy wasn't so fortunate. My wife sang at her funeral, and until a week ago their house had stood, empty, for seven years.

There but for the grace of God, we say, but grace can be a tricky concept. Bad things do happen to good people, and errors in judgment have ripples of consequence that vary widely. My little misadventure turned out all right. There's a big hole next door.

I await my new neighbors with the same anticipation I do the sun, grounded in reality but hopeful. Maybe they'll be friendly. Maybe they'll have kids. Maybe they'll leave their windows open from time to time and laughter will drift across the lawn. It won't be the same, of course, but it'll be nice to hear again anyway.

On The Road

"Let's take the Rambler," he said, and I laughed so he said it again. "Let's take the Rambler to Portland. Let's take a road trip."

We'd been planning this for months, my friend Dave and I, our annual summer reunion of high school friends in Oregon. We'd decided to take the train and it left in less than an hour, and we already had our tickets.

"What are you talking about?" I think I said, with maybe some other words added in there for effect. Words we tend to think of as Anglo-Saxon but really aren't.

"I may not have it next year, so the Rambler needs at least one road trip. C'mon, it'll be fun."

He'd bought this car, a 1963 Rambler, a few months before when he spotted it for sale on the street. Dave has an eclectic appreciation of old stuff. He's got an incredible collection of pulp fiction from the 1950s. He's an amateur student of interior design of the 1970s. He's written articles on European spy movies from the 1960s. Eclectic is maybe not the right word.

I understand passion and spontaneity. I outgrew them. It sounded so important to him, though, and one way or the other we needed to get to Oregon, so there we were, driving south on Highway 99 early on a Sunday morning in a car barely younger than we were. A car that would have graduated high school in

1981. A car that should have known better than to drive to Portland at its age.

It must have been sweet in 1963, though. Automatic transmission, bucket seats, a V8 under the hood. It had an AM radio and wind wings and separate ashtrays for the driver and the front seat passenger. This was a car made for a country that smoked a lot.

"Does it have a name?" I asked, and I was joking. "Florinda," he said, and he wasn't, so I just looked out the window as we passed the train station. I've only been on a train a couple of times, and that was at Disneyland. I had been looking forward to it.

There was something about Florinda, though, something about taking her on the open road that seeped up from the seats and murmured of Ken Kesey and Jack Kerouac, something that slowly made me smile. Here we are, I thought, two guys in a 40-year-old car, driving the highway on the road to Portland, and suddenly I'm laughing in spite of myself, enjoying the novelty of it.

There was a cinematic overlay here, a playacting quality, and we stopped at a gas station in the middle of nowhere and I could tell Dave was feeling it too. "I'll fill her up," he said, "and you go inside and rob the place."

We turned on the radio and there was Nat King Cole, and we drove past farms and fields and it could have been a new car and another age.

There is no safe time, I know, no placid year free from worry. If we are driving a new Rambler in the summer of 1963, already

16,000 "advisors" are in Vietnam, a civil rights march on Washington looms, and plans are in the works for President Kennedy to take a trip to Texas in the fall. "You're heading into crazy country," a friend warns him.

But we were heading into God's country, and that big engine purred down the interstate at 80 like it was no big deal. She tended to shimmy on wide turns but she stayed cool and it was cool, this car, and I decided then that a train was too sedate for a spontaneous and passionate guy like me.

We stopped at a diner, a small town restaurant boasting on its billboard that Jack Benny and Elvis had eaten there. Dave had steak and eggs and I had the Jack Benny Burger, which was neither spartan nor particularly cheap. It was good, though, and even if the waitress didn't call us "Hon" the service was excellent. For all I knew Elvis was in the back, finishing off my fries.

We came home two days later to traffic and a tanker truck burning in Issaquah. The stock market was tumbling, major companies were shuddering from the top down, and a little girl had been kidnapped in California. We were in crazy country again, but we'd been somewhere else for a while.

We live in troubling times and there's no getting around it, but I'll tell you what: If somebody offers you a ride in a Rambler, it's worth thinking about. It's an old-fashioned car, one with room to stretch your legs all the way out. Tune the radio to Nat King Cole, pop the wind wings, and smoke 'em if you got 'em. There's still summer, and friends, and open highways to be grateful for, and a road trip never hurt anybody.

Do Not Pass "Go"

It's a bitter pill to swallow, particularly at 4:30 a.m. on your 44th birthday. The prednisone tablet is small and thin, but if I let it linger on my tongue more than half a second I'm tasting it the rest of the morning. A reminder, and happy birthday to me. Not that I'm depressed.

Prednisone is strong medicine, intended to speed healing to muscles that have gotten irritated and aren't going to take it anymore. I saw a doctor at the walk-in clinic after suffering (not in silence either, not me) for a few days. I described how the pain started in my shoulder and then wandered down the outside of my arm, stopping to dance a bit at my elbow and making me wonder if I really needed an elbow all that much anyway, and then proceeded down to my hand, where it made my fingers jump from time to time. Sometimes my whole hand would jerk and flutter involuntarily and I'd watch it flap around, feeling like an interior decorator making a big presentation.

My regular doctor was booked up, which was probably a good thing as she would have just laughed at me. She does that a lot; it's a style thing, a casualness that I appreciate, but this was big-time pain and this guy was serious about it. He probed and took me through different positions, and then announced that it was probably my neck.

I was ignorant enough to think that if my shoulder hurt, it was a shoulder problem, but he mentioned referred pain and spastic rhomboids so I kept my mouth shut. He gave me prescriptions for the prednisone along with a muscle relaxant and a pain medication, so my birthday started with a steroid jolt and then a loosey-goosey feeling in my arms and legs, and finally a narcotic fuzz that lasted through the day. Birthdays used to be better than this.

I didn't tell the doctor about the Monopoly game. He seemed in a hurry and it would have been awkward anyway. My son got this "Star Trek" version of Monopoly, where you buy starships instead of hotels and Park Place is some weird planet and your pieces are aliens (I think one of them was a Spastic Rhomboid, come to think of it). You still went to Jail and passed Go, though, and I did a lot of reaching across the table to move and that was probably it.

I saw a woman once wearing a tee shirt that said, "Oh, no. I'm 40 and I forgot to have a baby!" There are no instructions for creeping into middle age but we expect them to be there, and then when they're not we realize we've missed some stuff. Wasn't there something about flossing? I vaguely remember comments about stretching and dollar cost averaging and not voting for Democrats, but I guess I wasn't paying attention. I was 22 yesterday, after all, and the chances of being 44 seemed pretty remote. Now, suddenly, I'm here and I realize that optimistically half my life is over, gone, kaput, and I've yet to write a novel or see Spain and I have to use caution with board games.

"The great thing about getting older," author Madeleine L'Engle wrote, "is that you don't lose all the other ages you've been." This is true, I think, but there's still a lot of condescension to deal with. A friend of mine once said that getting older meant always imagining your 14-year-old self standing over your shoulder, smirking and disappointed at how you turned out.

On the other hand, when I was 14 I was trying to make the freshman football team and my greatest desire was to gain weight. So maybe I'm OK.

Oh, it's just another birthday, and I'm optimistic enough to dream that I can reverse the years of sedentary life. Maybe you'll see me out there, along the side of the road, jogging so slowly that squirrels are rolling on the ground, holding their stomachs as they laugh at the image. I'll be wearing baggy sweat pants and a tee shirt that says, "Oh, no. I'm 44 and I forgot to exercise!" I'll be breathing hard. My hand may be doing a little dance.

But give me some room. Acknowledge my effort. Envision my potential. Have some pity.

Or, better yet, just run me over. You might be doing us all a favor, sparing us the sight of one more middle-aged man trying to reclaim his youth and his thin thighs. I had my chance, after all, and I could have flossed if I'd really wanted to. It's all about choices, and if you land on Park Place you need to buy it then. Passing Go is never guaranteed. Not that I'm depressed.

The Stuff That Dreams Are Made Of

I dream a lot, or else I remember my dreams more than most people. The subject has come up in groups often enough for me to accept this as fact, although I can't say that it makes me feel special or even interesting. Mostly I feel weird about it, as if I were double jointed or had three kidneys or a bad cowlick that no one could fix. You never know what you'll end up with but I'd rather not talk about it.

I have to sometimes, though, so my wife and I have developed shorthand to let me get things off my chest and spare her from speculating on my sanity. "I had The Pool Dream last night," I tell her, or The Basement Dream or The Freeway Dream or The Graduation Dream, and she nods thoughtfully and then announces that she really, really has to jump in the shower now. She's very clean.

The other night, I told her, it started out as a version of that old reliable, The Actor's Nightmare, but then it turned into a Kurt Dream. It had been a while.

I met Kurt Streif in the seventh grade, but we didn't become good friends until our sophomore year in high school, when he did an extraordinary thing. I was a little shy and insecure (imagine that), and Kurt decided I should audition for "The Christmas Carol" at school. He was shorter and sort of roly-poly, but his will was strong and he pretty much forced me. As it turned out, I got a part and he didn't, but if this seemed unfair to him he never let on.

He picked me up every morning to drive me to school, and usually dropped me back at the end of the day. We became fixtures at each other's home, allowed to walk in without knocking and search through the refrigerator without asking. We double dated to the prom and cruised around on Friday nights when we had nothing better to do.

We roomed together for a couple of years in college, and then I got flaky and he met new friends and we just drifted. We kept in touch, and he was always around to help me work on my car or give me a lift somewhere, but life happened in there somewhere. One day he knocked on my door unexpectedly and said, "I heard you got married," and I had a flash then, a sense of something not right about this, but I just hemmed and hawed, embarrassed.

A couple of years later we met at a wedding reception. He was feeling melancholy; all his friends were getting married, and he held my six-month-old daughter in his arms and said, "I should know her." He was sensing it, too, friendship tossed in the trash can as if it were useless just because we grew up.

I saw him about 10 years ago, at a retirement party for a mutual professor. He had mellowed; his edges were softer and he smiled more. He'd married a woman with two children and he was solicitous of them, making sure they were comfortable at a gathering of strangers. I showed him pictures of my kids and house and he nodded and laughed at my stories.

This is the Kurt in my dreams, by the way. Calm, peaceful, always happy to see me, and no matter how hard I try to explain he never seems to quite grasp the fact that he's dead.

"I have some bad news," I heard on the phone three years ago this month. I knew that when I heard his voice, an old college friend from years ago, but I didn't know what and I didn't know how bad. Having a good heart doesn't necessarily mean it won't be a diseased one. You never know what you'll end up with.

Accepted and expected futures are nice dreams but still dreams. We put off calling or writing letters, we leave things unsaid for a more convenient time, some reunion when we toast our memories and say, "I never told you this, but…" and then an old friend drops dead and we sit at the computer and weep. We wear the chains we forge in life, these unspoken things, and they weigh us down with regret. So I have these dreams.

I'm always in some sort of trouble in them. I've run out of gas or gotten lost, and suddenly there's Kurt, standing by his truck, smiling. He tells me to get in and he'll give me a ride, and I do and I relax then, knowing I'm safe and heading for home. It's a comforting dream, a peaceful one with a familiar feel, and it's marred only by the fact that I always wake up before I have a chance to thank him.

The Other Chuck

He is tall and lean, cynical and, at the moment, mad as hell. He was then my age now, although any other resemblance is purely coincidental and not likely to be found anyway. If I looked that good in a loincloth, I'd be wearing one going out to get the mail every day. Trust me.

I watch from the darkness of the backseat of our family car, nestled on pillows and full of popcorn. He plots and eludes and fights, and when he's finally captured his voice comes back, raspy and powerful. "Get your stinking paws off me, you damn dirty ape!" I know it by heart.

This was my introduction to Charlton Heston, "Planet Of The Apes" in a drive-in when I was 10. It remains a favorite, and I watched it the other night with my son. It holds up well, partly due to crisp, spare direction but mostly to its leading man.

I watched it for the sake of nostalgia, to wander back a bit, to relive a memorable experience. I watched it to think about Charlton Heston, and to see if I remembered that famous line correctly, and to wonder if there will reach a point when he doesn't.

I was sort of inexplicably saddened by the announcement last Friday that he may have Alzheimer's disease. It's a horrible illness, but even given a decent human tendency to grieve over a stranger's misfortune there are degrees of separation. I don't know him.

I know something about him, though, and I've followed his career, and my interest perplexes my friends. He was at the top of his game for almost 25 years, but he hasn't starred in a successful film since "Gray Lady Down" in 1978, and over the past couple of decades he's been most prominent for his active, and increasingly strident, interest in political matters. Conservative politics.

We're not allowed to do this, of course, separate out political philosophy. Belief in an activist or limited federal government, the most basic definition of liberalism or conservatism in our time, has become an all-encompassing statement of what kind of people we are, particularly to those of the opposite viewpoint.

Are you a conservative? Then you're a racist, homophobic, money-grubbing, earth-polluting, God-distorting, orphan-tossing elitist. A liberal? You're a naïve, atheistic, socially destructive, tax-loving, agenda-pushing, simple-minded fool. God help your kids, having to live with you (my kind of God, that is).

So what's the thing with Charlton Heston and me? I don't agree with him politically for the most part. And aside from "Apes," "Touch Of Evil" and "Will Penny," I actually find his films mostly forgettable.

He was the right man for the right time, though, a big guy with a broken nose and a booming voice, who seemed faintly Roman or maybe Greek (actually a Scot) and fit the Fifties love of epics. He straddled two eras in movie making and could pass for classical or contemporary. He was comfortable on a horse, and more so with Shakespeare. He had a nice run.

I think he's disingenuous with his history. Even in his statement last week, he said, "I'm still the same man that JFK, Dr. King, and Ronald Reagan knew." Oh, well, please. He goes back a long way with Reagan, but by his own account he met Kennedy for a total of two minutes, a movie star appearance.

He participated with a group of Hollywood types in the March On Washington in 1963, but that was about the extent of his civil rights involvement and to morph that into "I marched with Dr. King," as he does, smells a little dishonest.

I understand this, though. He fights being labeled and wants to be seen as an independent thinker, no matter how in lockstep he marches with his ideological equals. There is more to a life, and a man, than a vote or two. There are fine children, and a marriage of over 50 years, and a work ethic unrivaled in his business.

He served his country in war and then as a celebrity, making countless good will trips around the globe to promote American culture and values. During the Vietnam War, he traveled to Southeast Asia twice, alone so he could go where the big shows couldn't, back where the soldiers needed a face from home. He stood up to be counted and he made his views known, and if I disagree with his opinions it doesn't change the fact that I admire him for being consistent.

And for more than that. For being a good and decent man, for being a responsible citizen, and for giving us all some moments of pleasure. All he wanted was an actor's life, and if he got more than he bargained for he also has a final battle to fight. I doubt that he'll take it lying down. Not my Chuck.

A Dumb Blond Joke

Early Man had the blues. He sat on the grass, half-heartedly tossing rocks into the tar pit and sighing a lot. Early Dog sat at his feet, watching his morose master. Early Woman crawled out of the cave and observed the situation. "What's the problem?" she asked.

"I'm middle-aged and there's no excitement anymore," said Early Man. "I might as well throw myself into the pit along with the other animals. My life is over."

Early Woman laughed. "What are you talking about? You're 16. You're in the prime of life." Early Man shook his head. "If I'm lucky and don't get eaten, I'll have at most 20 years left. What's the point?"

"Oh, come on," said Early Woman. "We've got this nice cave, and Early Boy and Early Girl, and our friends. And," she added slyly, "the other females say that of all the men, you smell the best. Go out and hunt or gather or something. You'll feel better." Early Man sighed again but got to his feet and wandered off.

Two hours later, he burst into the cave with a grin on his face. "Well, you look in a better mood," said Early Woman. "Did you snag a saber-tooth?" Early Man shook his head. "Nope."

"Let me guess," said Early Woman. "A bear?" Another shake. "One of those furry things with the big horns? A raccoon? A big fish? An armful of nuts?" Early Man laughed.

Early Woman frowned. "It's almost time for dinner. What DID you bring home?" Early Man grinned even broader.

"A Porsche," he said.

It's a story as old as time itself, proving once again that God created man, thought about it a bit, then decided to make some improvements. Women reach middle age, have a couple of hot flashes, then get Master's degrees or start businesses or run for office. Men, on the other hand, sulk for a long time and then buy Viagra by the case and try to fit into pants that apparently were made for another species.

Even those of us who are well adjusted, successful, or too afraid of needles to get earrings are suspect. I'm sure if Bill Gates were to add to his collection of cars and chose one that happened to be a red convertible, Melissa would be on the phone to friends in a second, talking about her husband "going through a phase." We're all guilty of having midlife crises until proven innocent.

So I guess I should explain why I'm now a blond.

See, I have these rules about life, and as long as I follow them I stay out of trouble. They're mostly common sense. For example, rule #11 states, "If your plans for the evening include drinking beer and trimming your beard, do the beard first." See? Common sense.

Another rule is that under no circumstances am I to allow the women in my life to change my appearance. They mean well, but really we're just big Ken dolls to them, and they'd dearly love to dress us up and brush our hair. It never occurs to them that we are, theoretically anyway, real people.

I was tired the other night, though. I came upstairs after a long day and found my daughter putting blond streaks into my son's hair (12-year-old boys haven't learned the rule yet). "Do your dad's hair!" my wife helpfully called out, and in my defenseless state I suddenly found myself sitting on a stool in the kitchen while my daughter brushed chemicals into my scalp.

I used to be blond. My hair started turning into this ugly dead brown color about the time I started a business and began working 14-hour days, never seeing the light of day. So I admit I wasn't all that resistant to having a couple of highlights here and there. Maybe it would look good. It couldn't hurt, could it? And it washes right out, doesn't it? Doesn't it?

You breaks the rules, you pays the price. Twenty minutes later I stared in the mirror and staring back was a 40-ish version of Robert Redford (it's an excellent mirror). I was surfer blond. California blond. Embarrassingly blond.

I take full responsibility, but I want to state for the record (I hope one of you is writing this down) that my new look has nothing to do with a longing for my youth, or middle-age gloominess or any desire at all to look better. It has everything to do with being a wimp. And if you spot me around town and notice that I look slightly different, or (more likely) am wearing a hat pulled down low over my head, you now have an explanation.

I should also explain why last Saturday night I ended up having to shave off my beard. But you can probably figure that one out.

The Measure Of A Man

I'm a Chuck and always have been, and it's probably too late to change at this point even if I wanted to. It's a name I share with my father, but it was given to me by my mother during a moment when Dad was out of the hospital room. Which seems a dirty trick, looking back, but it's mine now so I'm stuck with it.

I am, of course, officially a Charles, but if you call me that you are probably either trying to persuade me to refinance my mortgage or writing me a speeding ticket. I picked up the phone the other day, though, and heard "Charles?" spoken with sort of an upward lilt that suggested to me immediately that I possibly was in big trouble. Or I would have been was I still a college freshman, as that's when I heard it a lot.

Clifford White, Ph.D., Professor Emeritus of Northern Arizona University, was the head of the theater department there in 1976, which is when I met him. Now that I look back, I seem to remember being pretty aimless back then, not sure what it was I was interested in, and I ended up at NAU mostly because I couldn't think of anything better to do. Not that I would mention any of this to Cliff.

Not that I would have called him Cliff, either, not back then. Things were already starting to loosen up in the '70s and a familiarity between student and professor wasn't uncommon, but in the World According To Dr. White someone was always the grownup, and he knew who it was.

He was 51 then, tall and imposing, with a booming voice and perfect diction. Voice and Diction was one of his classes, along with Oral Interpretation, and he not only set an example, he was the example. "Do you mean PITCH-er or PICT-ure, Charles?" and I never could please him. He would finally throw up his hands in frustration, or else slap his knee and roar at the look on my face.

I don't know when it happened, sometime in the 1980s probably, but a liberal arts education began to be viewed as a lark, as an escape from real life, and serious and ambitious people went to college to get a job, a high-paying good job, and the sooner the better. It seemed that we became a country of business majors and then MBAs, all education being preparatory for a specialized career. Anything else was a waste of time.

Those of us who majored in theater, though, or music or art or literature know differently. Sure, specialization would come later, as interests focused and necessities entered the picture, but I suspect most of us would never trade those few years we spent delving into the minds of the ones who created our culture and civilization. You can always get your MBA; you can never be 18 again and read "The Tempest" for the first time, and be taught by those who love it just as much.

Cliff called the other day and we talked for 45 minutes, and I was surprised, in a very hectic week, that I found so much joy from hearing his voice. At 76, it is still strong and resonant, and he brims over with news and thoughts and concerns and questions. He was a taskmaster and a man to be feared if your paper was late or you weren't off book at the scheduled time, but he loved his students, each and every one, and there are some of us he stays in touch with. He and his wife, Doris, were surrogate parents to many, guiding us through our first steps into adulthood.

At his retirement party in 1992, he seemed genuinely surprised to see students return from all over the country to wish him well. After speeches and tributes and a skit or two, poking a little fun at our Dr. White, he spoke of many things but mostly us. He had regrets that he perhaps didn't spend enough time with his kids. "I was spending it with other people's kids," he said.

I've seen him regularly over the years, including last summer, when he and Doris helped me show my son the halls I walked when I was not much older than he is. There were classrooms, and makeup rooms and costume rooms, and finally the theater that now bears Clifford White's name.

I have tremendous affection for him, this man who helped shape my life. I once stood on a stage at 19, unable to please him, frustrated by the whole thing. I finally asked him what it was he wanted me to do.

"Do better," he said, and God love him for that. I will never be too old to need to hear it, especially from him.

The First Day

My wife tells me I'm not a doctor. She says this all the time. It might seem strange, but at least it provokes conversation between the two of us, and that's always good. You can try it yourself. Go up to your spouse and say, "You're not a machinist" or "You're not a flamenco dancer." It's fun. Stay away from sensitive subjects.

My wife says this, though, because I tend to avoid going to the doctor for what I consider minor aches and pains, most of which she thinks are signs of a heart attack. She worries about me, and not without reason, but I hate to waste time and money. And I'm always right, anyway.

The other day, though, I had a medical situation that concerned me. Sometimes when this happens I will call my friend Steve Hammond, who actually is a physician, but I decided against it because (A) he's a busy man, and (B) I'm pretty sure he suspects I think I'm a doctor, too.

So I called a nurse hotline instead and, after looking through the guidelines, this woman announced that it was a good thing I wasn't dead. I agreed, but after some discussion I ended up in the emergency room and then having a CAT scan. This was negative, which (but of course) I knew already. It did not show signs of intelligence either, but sometimes it won't.

It reminded me, though, of how quickly cutting edge technology becomes commonplace. In 1977 I had a summer job working in the radiology department of a large hospital, and their newest toy was a CAT scanner. It was a big deal then, as was an MRI machine 10 years later. Now they're everywhere, and I assume home versions are in the works.

I like technology toys. In 1979 I bought my first VCR (it was called a Video Tape Recorder back then, and it cost me $600. That was half price, too, and a blank tape cost $20 and there were no movies to rent. In case my age has not been firmly established yet).

In 1984, when my wife was pregnant with our first child and we lived far away from all relatives, I decided that we needed a video camera so we could send tapes to family. As I recall, we paid $1600 for this bulky unit, and it's possible, given our absolute incompetence on credit matters, that we're still paying for it.

I got a lot of use out of it, though, mostly recording my baby daughter when she was doing fascinating things, like sleeping and/or going to sleep. When she started kindergarten I recorded the first day, and I've kept up the practice.

This week I got number 13. Thirteen first days of school, all taped and stored. There's a 5-year-old there, excited about starting school, and an 8-year-old who still has trouble with the "R" sound, and a 12-year-old who finds the whole thing annoying, and now a 17-year-old who has her own sense of history and would not allow me to miss it.

In T. H. White's wonderful book, "The Once And Future King," there's a point toward the beginning when the young Arthur wanders into the woods and meets Merlin for the first time. The wizard momentarily sheds a tear or two at the meeting. "So little time left," he murmurs, for Merlin lives his life backwards, aging from the future into the past. His first glimpse of Arthur is also his last, and his memories are of the things yet to be.

I know the feeling. At 44, I remain my age and still wander back in time through the videos. This young woman in my life, nearing 18 and starting her senior year in high school, is there on the screen, a few minutes old and screaming like crazy as her mother laughs with the joy of it. The boy who now almost stands eye to eye with me is there, shoving chocolate cake into his mouth from his highchair, marking his first birthday.

I peruse the past and I know the future. It's just a series of stages, after all. My wife and I have accepted this and look forward to the time when the kids are gone, off on their own lives, our duty mostly complete, but still. First days of school are nearing a close. So little time left.

I record their lives for them to remember, I say, but I know better. I will sit in the darkened den years from now, watching my videos. I'll come out of the room, red eyed, and my wife will worry that I'm having a heart attack. You're a silly woman, I'll say, knowing my pain is ordinary. A life, as the Irish say, but it's my life, and I have the pictures to prove it.

Try To Remember

My father doesn't remember his fifth birthday, but he knows what day of the week it was. Even if sixty years have diminished its memory a bit, that particular Sunday is hard to forget, December 7, 1941.

My wife's parents remember their 17th wedding anniversary. They celebrated by going out to dinner in an unusually subdued Dallas that Friday night, November 22, 1963.

My nephew turned 21 last September 11. It's a big birthday, our statutory introduction to adulthood, but it probably wasn't his favorite. He'll remember it, though.

The calendar is arbitrary, invented by humans in a futile attempt to gain some control over relentless time. This day we call September 11 has no relation to the last one, other than the position of the earth in regard to the rest of the universe and maybe the color of the leaves on the trees. We mark it, though, and we will in the years to come. How we do so is still a question.

Pearl Harbor Day is a muted memory now, worthy of only a few words on the nightly news. In late November there might be a picture of Kennedy family members in Arlington Cemetery in the paper, but the rest of us will pay little attention. No one remembers the Maine anymore, or Shiloh. We are a positive people and prefer to dwell on happier things. National tragedies become dim, left for only the survivors to mark.

This one is still fresh, though. We have the images still, the planes and the smoke and the terror in the streets of Manhattan. We think of the smashed walls of the Pentagon and the last words from the passengers of Flight 93. We still hear the murmurs of the broadcasters who, like us, could not find the words to express their shock.

I always think of the ones who waited that day. They were at work or got there quickly, professional and prepared. They went over triage protocols and set up equipment. Doctors and nurses, support personnel and specialists all over New York were ready that morning, ready to serve and save whom they could. They were waiting for survivors. They waited a long time.

Time passes. We will grieve a little less this year. We will rebuild. We will prepare for the future. We will have speeches and sermons. We will still have birthdays and anniversaries. As I say, we are a positive people.

Every Veteran's Day, my father-in-law goes to the local cemetery and puts little American flags on the gravestones. Every year, this is what he does. He served in North Africa and Europe, two straight years on the front lines, and he won't talk about the war much but he remembers, and this is how he marks his day. He is a survivor.

We are the survivors of September 11, you and I. The 3000 who died that day are mourned by their families and friends and we can't truly share their pain, but we remember. We rediscovered our patriotism that day, not the marching band kind or the flag-waving kind, not the superficial kind or the shrill, bitter kind that peers suspiciously at those who dissent, but the best kind.

We remembered that we are a community, with more in common than we thought. We share a history and a dream, and our disagreements, faults, prejudices and preferences were set aside because our family was suffering.

We took it personally, as families will, and we reacted personally. We gave blood and money, we lit candles and placed flowers at fire stations. We remembered who we were, and faced with evil we found goodness in ourselves.

I wish for my nephew a happier birthday this year. He's grown into a good man with a big heart, like his father, and 22 is a nice age to be in any time.

I wish for the rest of us a day to remember, to pray for the victims and their families, to honor those who serve us, and to think about the nature of a national community.

We have been hurt, but we've cleared the rubble. We've been connected by tragedy, and if life is back to normal now we've still glimpsed a sense of family, and that's changed us.

Families are rainy day friends, arguing and fighting over simple things but always there when another is in trouble. It's good to try to remember where we were and how we felt, for that was the best of us.

There's no need to wait for survivors. They're all around us, hurt or suffering, hungry or homeless. If we remember who we are, then we are compelled to help them. And we will, we always have. We just forget sometimes. Which is why we have calendars, and why we mark certain days, and why we should.

Suffer The Little Children

My daughter has a long memory. Although she was probably 4 or 5 at the time, she's never forgotten this and probably never will. She carries no physical scars, but parents can never know for certain what emotional ones our children might bear.

It was toward the end of a long, exhausting day. I was standing at the sink, washing dishes, and Beth, as I recall, was practicing her newfound skill of sarcasm. What exactly provoked my outburst I've forgotten, but something snapped and in a moment of anger I whirled around toward her. I can still hear her scream in surprise and shock as she saw, hurtling toward her from across the room, a slightly damp dishtowel. It glanced off her shoulder and fell to the floor. I still feel a little guilty.

If it seems I'm making light of a serious subject, it's only because at this moment it's my only defense against some very ugly feelings. I watched last week, as did many of you, the surveillance camera footage of Madelyne Gorman Toogood looking around furtively and then pummeling her 4-year-old daughter in a parking lot in Indiana. It was "graphic and unsettling," as they warned us beforehand. It wasn't enough of a warning for me.

Aside from a few light swats on a heavily diapered rear end, more of an attention getter than as punishment, I've never hit my children. There's nothing noble about this, any more than never killing my parents or never setting my neighbor's house on fire.

There are things you don't do, in my world, and hitting children is one of them.

It happens all the time, though, just rarely for the cameras. Some of it is legitimized by convention, the mother tiger cuffing her cub with a paw to correct behavior. This is "corporal punishment," legalized hitting, and yeah, I've had the discussion so many times I have no desire to go there. It's really a philosophical issue, a parenting choice, and if I disagree it doesn't mean I'm calling the cops if you turn your kid over your knee dispassionately for the sake of discipline. Just not my style. That's not what I'm talking about.

What I'm talking about is the opposite of dispassionate. It's what I see in the grocery store. The little girl is bopping around, picking at the candy the store has so thoughtfully placed within reach at the check-out counter. Her mother finally has enough and grabs the kid by the arm, jerks her around, shakes her, gets in her face and hisses threats, her mouth twisted with rage. Sometimes I catch her eye and she gives me a "what are you looking at?" glance. Sometimes I catch the little girl's eye. I try not to think about what happens at home. Maybe nothing.

And maybe Ms. Toogood's 4-year-old daughter was being a brat on a bad day. Maybe her mother was driven to the point of extreme frustration. Maybe she felt like punching and slapping her child. Maybe the difference between her and us, the difference that led to what happened that day in the backseat of her van, is slight and marginal, just a matter of timing and life experience. I have a feeling it's less than we're comfortable imagining. So I've never hit my kids. I didn't trust myself to be dispassionate.

"My child shouldn't pay for a mistake I made," she said on Saturday night, frustrated by the refusal of authorities to let her daughter stay with relatives instead of strangers. Well, she's obviously not an educated person, ungrammatical and inarticulate, but at that moment I was genuinely moved and I wanted to reach out to her through the TV and wring her ignorant neck.

A mistake is when you type "they're" and mean "their." A mistake is bringing home the wrong kind of spaghetti sauce. A mistake is being caught at first base leaning the wrong way. Even a stupid person knows it's wrong to beat up a 4-year-old girl. It's not a mistake, and it's not a "wrong choice." It's not a choice at all.

I have seen obviously unskilled parents. I've seen bad behavior by adults. I used to see a paraeducator at my child's school just deliberately humiliate and torment little first-graders, puffing herself up as she strutted around the campus. There are issues of power, and cycles of abuse and bad daddies, etc. A lot of this explains a lot of things. Understanding is not the same as excusing.

There is no excuse for hurting a child. Just my opinion, of course. I have no idea what's going to happen to this woman, but I have an opinion on that, too. Oh, you betcha. Make no mistake about it.

And The Winner Is...

There is a young woman in, say, Kansas, playing the lead in the local community theater production of "Our Town," and she has a fantasy all her own. It's snowing, or raining, or whatever the weather does in Kansas, and by an odd coincidence Steven Spielberg is passing through her small town, stranded and in need of a little evening entertainment. A star is born, and so on.

She's a stock character, this woman, in the drama of foolish dreams, along with the mailroom worker and garage band and salesman who writes at night. They dream long after their time is up, older and fatter and surrounded by kids and bills and weeds. A majority of men who played high school sports, a survey revealed, believe they could have made it in the pros if they'd just been given a chance. I coulda been a contender, Charlie.

I am, of course, immune from such fantasies, which didn't stop my heart from jumping a bit when my wife told me about the message on our answering machine. "Someone wants to give you an award," she said in an unbelieving tone, as if somebody had just offered me a job as a heart surgeon or a Chippendale's dancer. Nineteen years of marriage can make a realist out of anyone but hey, it could happen, and by the way thanks for the support.

The message was muffled but I could make it out. Some guy in Washington, D.C. working for Tom DeLay and congressional

Republicans was telling me I'd received a National Leadership Award, and they needed to talk to me about a press release. Call as soon as you get this message, etc.

Recognition is the phone call that never comes, and we get used to it and manage to survive, but here it was. I was finally being honored for all those years, all that effort, all that work I did on...national leadership, or something, and it was a proud moment. "You're not even a Republican," my wife said. "I TRANSCEND politics," I replied and played the message again.

I wasn't born yesterday, of course, and caution being the better part of valor (i.e., national leadership) I decided to consult Mr. Google first. Typing in "National Leadership Award" got me hundreds of entries, but refining the search a bit (Try this at home! It's fun! And educational!) by adding the words "Tom DeLay" I got my answer.

"ABC News: Questions About GOP Fundraising Tactics" was the very first site that popped up, but there were lots of them, telling the same story. It was the classic bait-and-switch: Small business owners are called and told they're being honored for service to their community, but in order to receive the award (and to receive access to important legislators) a small contribution of $350 or $500 is required to cover costs, etc.

Obviously it works to some extent, because my Internet search also came up with several newspaper articles about how so-and-so had been honored with a National Leadership Award by the Republican National Congressional Committee. Appealing to greed has always been a successful tactic for con artists of all sorts; vanity seems a promising target, too. So I guess Tom DeLay should be proud.

I was going to play the game, call them and listen to their pitch and them self-righteously denounce their deception and get some good quotes, etc. I just didn't have the stomach for it, and the ethics sort of bothered me. So for all I know, despite the articles that described almost word for word the message left on my answering machine, it could have been on the up and up. Maybe the RNCC really did want to honor me for running a small business that, by the way, has been defunct for nearly two years. It could happen.

The scene in the taxi from "On The Waterfront" is one of the most famous in movie history, and when asked about it years later Marlon Brando shrugged it off. It was actor proof, he said, and I know what he means. The feeling that we could have been more successful, more famous, more honored, if only the breaks had gone our way or someone had recognized our talent must lie close to the surface in us, lurking behind the smile and apparent satisfaction with our lives.

I slunk back into the living room to tell my wife the bad news. It wasn't a surprise to her, of course. As I say, 19 years can make you a realist about your spouse. I was sort of moping, I guess, because she finally asked me what was wrong. I did my best Brando imitation. "Don't you see? I coulda been somebody...I coulda been a contender."

She patted me on the shoulder. "Of course you could have," she said, but, you know. In a nice way.

A Message For Mrs. Kurtenbach

The first day of October was also the first day of autumn, although it took a brisk walk around Lake Serene for me to realize it. There are those of you who will argue with me, you purists, and you'll talk about equinoxes and solstices and apogees and such. Shut up.

It was sharp and sunny and cold, and I came inside from my walk and yelled upstairs to my wife. "Hey!" I said. "You know what? It's fall!" She agreed with me, so there you go.

Spring is when a young man falls in love, but fall is when he gets serious about it. He knows that winter looms and his heart heads for commitment, for comfort and warm bodies and long nights. I have a lovely story to tell you about this, but first I have to explain about sponge puppets.

A sponge puppet, oddly enough, is a puppet made out of a sponge. You tie a rubber band around the top third to make the head, slip a piece of fabric under the rubber band to form a cape or a dress, then draw on facial features with a marking pen (nothing will stick to sponges; not glue, not tape, nothing). You then punch through two holes for your fingers, which become the puppet's arms. If you leave your fingers in the holes long enough, they will turn blue and then fall off.

I was making sponge puppets the other day with three five-year-old girls, whose spiritual care had been entrusted to me for 45 minutes on a Sunday morning. The plan was to use the puppets to act out the story of Noah and the Ark, but the idea of God flooding the world to rid it of wickedness seemed a little dark for these sunny faces, so we mostly just tried to name all the animals in the world and worked with sponges.

The conversation wandered a bit, from "The Little Mermaid" to dogs that chewed up Barbie dolls, and then to their schools and kindergarten teachers. "My teacher is Mrs. Kurtenbach," one of them said, and after a few questions I walked to the blackboard and proceeded to draw a really ugly map of the United States, which the girls found hilarious. I was happy to be entertaining, but what I was attempting to do, pretty unsuccessfully, was demonstrate how far away Washington was from Arizona, and how long ago 20 years was, and how it suddenly didn't seem that way at all.

I like coincidences. They make me wonder about destiny, and whether free will is an illusion or just a matter of perspective. They let me speculate on the idea of some master plan that, from time to time, we're allowed to see out of the corner of our eye. So I had fun explaining to this little girl that in the fall of 1982, in a small town 1400 miles away, her kindergarten teacher and I had played out a little drama on a college stage, and a bigger one off it.

The show was "Camelot." She wasn't yet a Kurtenbach then, but Mary Beth was a wonderful actress and singer, and she and I were cast as, respectively, Guinevere and King Arthur. The director had decided to double cast the main parts and the other guy playing Arthur was fairly short. Mary Beth is a tall woman, so she put her foot down and got me as her partner.

My girlfriend at that time would show up occasionally at rehearsals, aware that unplanned love or lust can be kindled in a play and keeping a watchful eye. This is sad and funny now, looking back. She had nothing to fear from Mary Beth, who I believe suspected that I was falling in love all right, but with the other Guinevere.

Our romance had been simmering for a while, this other woman and I, but given the right circumstances frustration can be fuel for love, and the fact that we were thwarted in our desire to perform together somehow provided the spark. Ten months later we were married and had moved to Seattle, and six years after that my wife, very pregnant with our second child, was visiting Mukilteo Presbyterian Church. She was standing in the crowded hall when her mother nudged her. "That tall woman over there is trying to get your attention," she said, and a neat little circle closed.

We see Mary Beth and Jeff Kurtenbach from time to time, and when we talk of our college days it's mostly just to laugh at how impossibly young we were and how funny it is that we all ended up in Washington. What a coincidence.

"I have a message for Mrs. Kurtenbach," I told the little girl, but a five-year-old's attention span is fleeting and it would have been complicated, anyway. It had to do with autumn, and theater, and romance and youth. It had to do with a mythical kingdom and real people's lives, and how chance plays a part in everything, and how there is always one brief, shining moment when we sort of understand that.

Evil in Our Mists

I moved to the Pacific Northwest in early October of 1983, so I know all about October.

October is a prankster, a con man, a swindler and a liar. If October tells you your shoe's untied, don't look down. If October whispers the name of a certain stock, don't buy it. If October shakes your hand, check your wallet.

October wants you to believe that the sunny days of summer weren't all that good, that August was too hot and it rained all of July. October wants you to appreciate the sparkling afternoons and the brisk mornings, the colors of the leaves and the taste of caramel apples. October wants to pull the wool over your eyes and at the same time yank your underwear up to your chest when you're not looking. October is leading you down a primrose lane, and at the end of that is November, so don't fall for it.

I thought about this last Thursday afternoon, driving down Beverly Park Road. It was sunny and clear, but to the west was something. Something different, a change of color in the sky. Not dark, not threatening. Just different.

This was the day they caught the sniper. Or snipers. And maybe they're innocent, but no one believes that. The terror that swept across Maryland and Virginia and Washington, D.C. for over a month ended with a whimper, some diligent police work and hubris on the part of the perpetrators, along with an observant trucker. Sleeping in their car, the bad guys became the unsuspecting targets they'd been threatening for weeks. And they got off easy, the freaks.

I walked outside at 6:45 that evening to head for the high school choir concert, and October had left me a business card. Fog, dense and rolling, covered the neighborhood, and it was too late to think about summer. But then, I'd seen it coming.

"It's smooky," my wife said, using the term my daughter coined when she was 6 years old and it was foggy. It's a good word. Part smoky and part spooky. Let it roll around your tongue for a while and you'll understand. It was a smooky night all right. I let my wife drive.

Fog is the prop in our film noir fantasies, the mist at the airport in Casablanca when Rick lets Ilsa go on her way and says he doesn't know much about being noble. Fog holds suspense and mystery, and the killer who strikes and disappears and leaves no clues.

Fog played no part back east when the sniper was killing at will. There was still the mystery, though, the sudden shots and the lack of shells and the occasional message. "I am God," one of them said. He struck and disappeared (and we knew it was a he, the way we know certain things in an uncertain world, not worth talking about), and while he wasn't God he was foggy and elusive, and reminded all of us, even those far away from the danger, that there was evil out there.

But we've always known it, right? Even if we stretch our rationalizing brains to explain every flaw, every mistake, listing our reasons from bad parenting to post-traumatic stress to depression, even if we allow perpetrators of evil to become understandable and even possibly worthy of forgiveness, we still recognize evil. It's always there, always has been and always will be.

Without evil there would be no good, or so they say. We need the contrasts, or else sunny days become common and not worth mentioning. So in a world where evil lies in the trunk and picks off children, I went to a high school choir concert and heard teenagers sing for the fun of it.

There were three choirs and two a cappella groups (and there's no bad day that can't be overcome by listening to a barbershop quartet; this is just truth, plain and simple), and they sang for 75 minutes and I hummed all the way home. We forgot to stop for milk, so I ran out later and got it, then stood in my driveway in the fog for a minute, hearing the evening's music run through my head once more.

The power of evil, someone once said, is not the act itself, but its ability to distract us from seeing the goodness of God and the joys of life. We have to fight it, or else what's the point? So we risk danger and expose ourselves, take some chances and let October deceive us every year. There are more important survival instincts than fear, I thought then, so I ended my day standing alone in my driveway on a smooky night, an easy target for a sniper, holding onto a gallon of milk and singing to myself in the fog like a fool.

It Is Right To Give Our Thanks And Praise

The autumn leaves pass by my window, and I know it's November.

They're lovely, light leaves that float down like auburn snow, and they remind me of creation and cycles of life and the fact that I really need to cut down that plum tree. Maybe next summer.

Raking leaves is a neighborly thing to do, particularly since a lot of them fall on my neighbor's lawn. It's a November duty, like cleaning the gutters or disconnecting garden hoses. It's also sentimental, bringing back memories of being a teenager and raking the leaves in the autumn, in between tossing a football or building the homecoming float. I rest my hand on the top of the rake and stand there, thinking. I decide I'm going to offer the next teenager who walks by $200 to rake them for me. A little sentiment goes a long way.

November is our month for reflecting, the month we give thanks for our abundance and usually give up hope for any playoff berth for the Seahawks. We get realistic in November, grateful for the important things.

Thanksgiving is our only holiday untouched by growing up; there's always been football and parades on TV, and the only change now is maybe how much time we spend in the kitchen. And that's the best part, anyway.

Preparing good food that will feed the people at your table three times over is a cozy penance for the past year's transgressions. It's a little work but never drudgery, and you can nip at the wine all you want and no one notices. Shove a turkey in the oven and baste it every 30 minutes and it'll turn out fine, or get fancy and rub an orange all over and stuff the cavity with lots of butter and sage and nuts and sausage. That's purely for your own benefit, though; it'll be mingled with mashed potatoes and fruit salad and you'll get few compliments because everyone's mouth is full.

Thanksgiving is for eating dishes you never think to eat any other time, all of them soaked in cups of gravy and whole sticks of melted butter. You ask who wants dessert and everyone defers, the Great Thanksgiving Lie, the pretense that eating four pounds of food at one sitting is enough for anybody, but by the end of the night there is one slice of cheesecake left and maybe a smidgen of whipped cream, and forget about the pumpkin pie.

Grace is always said at our Presbyterian table, although depending on the company we might sing a doxology, too. The prayer is sometimes practiced and fluent, and at other times delivered haltingly by a child who's not all that sure what to be grateful for, but knows God wants to hear something. Even the nonbelievers among us dip their heads, for Providence is intangible and unknown and you can never be too careful.

I'm grateful for friends who are near and family far away but connected via e-mail and free long distance on weekends and evenings. I'm grateful for neighbors who wave and talk and say nothing about the weeds I still haven't pulled. I'm grateful for the teachers who inspire my children. I'm grateful for leaders who inspire me, who remind me of my fortune in life and chide me about not doing more for those less fortunate. And I'm grateful to live where I do.

Thanksgiving is important to us in the Northwest. It was invented by Lewis and Clark, of course, in the fall of 1805 when they'd traveled into the unknown and lived to tell about it. They found no Northwest Passage but some friendly Tillamook and plenty of game, so they settled in for a winter of making salt and paying no sales tax.

Lewis suggested that perhaps taking a moment to give thanks for a safe journey was appropriate, and Clark ran with that and arranged for a parade and a touch football game on the banks of the Columbia, and there was turkey and broccoli-and-cheese casserole and leftovers to send to Thomas Jefferson.

They thanked Almighty God for deliverance and for this beautiful Northwest countryside, and they planted a plum tree to mark the day. Forty-five years later Arthur Denny took a clipping from that very tree and brought it up north, planting it in what would become my backyard, where it now sheds its leaves every November.

This is God's way of telling me to get some fresh air, I know, so I do. Raking leaves is a small price to pay for the grace of God, for the beauty of the land, the love of good friends and the luxury of second helpings. I am grateful for all of this, and for children and music and democracy, and for Northwest Novembers to remind me that I should be.

Keeping The Faith

I'd like to begin today, as I do in nearly every column, with a quote from Dolly Parton.

"I don't mind dumb blonde jokes," Dolly said, "because I know I'm not dumb, and because I also know I'm not blonde."

She's talking, of course, about guilt by association, that frustrating feeling we all have from time to time, knowing we're being judged and catalogued by sharing traits, beliefs, political philosophy, or affection for "Star Trek" with people we'd rather not share things with.

People who end sentences with prepositions, for example.

And, Lord, it's hard to be a Christian these days.

I try. I go to church every Sunday, where I hear homilies on hope and forgiveness, on judging not lest I be judged and on salvation through grace. I mingle with other members of the congregation and we talk about mission projects and youth ministry, and I leave in a good mood and then find I've been co-opted while I worshipped.

You can't pick your relatives, and likewise your brethren in faith, but sometimes it sure sounds like a nice idea. Christianity is the most widely practiced religion on the planet, in versatile and diverse ways. This is true in the United States, too, but to watch the news you'd think we were all like them.

We all know who they are, of course. They are Bob Jones University and the PTL Club. They are Jimmy Swaggart with his penchant for prostitutes and Jerry Falwell with his firm conviction that God hates liberals and told him this personally. They are the big hair people, the Religious Right, hyperactive and hypocritical, spewing hate and intolerance and political positions over the airwaves, all in the name of the Prince of Peace. They are my brothers and sisters in Christ, and they are also, occasionally, The Enemy.

They're a dangerous enemy, these Christian brethren of mine, and not to be taken lightly. They pick their targets carefully and stay on message. Eight years of Bill and Hillary sharpened their wits and filled their coffers.

Islam bashing is the latest sport for my fellow believers, and it's got the White House in full damage control mode. Last month President Bush hosted a Ramadan dinner for American Muslims, assuring them that he knew Islam was a "peaceful religion." Colin Powell made similar remarks a week later.

You have to give them credit. The Bush Administration, attempting to fight a war on terrorism and build a coalition for an invasion of Iraq, has gone out of its way to try to reassure the over one billion Muslims in the world that America has nothing against Islam. They've done everything but mention that the Oval Office windows point toward Mecca, and still the sense is of an issue that's out of control.

Falwell got up to speed quickly, calling Muhammad a "terrorist." Robertson talks on television of the inherent hate behind Islam. Franklin Graham has developed a nice rhythm, saying that Islam is a "violent" religion, apologizing, then saying it again. Read the Qur'an, he says. You'll see it's a violent book.

I know it's a dumb question, but do you suppose Franklin has ever read the Bible? I mean, really read it? The parts about plagues and murdering first-borns and dashing babies' skulls against rocks?

Has Falwell ever considered the notion that if Muhammad was a terrorist, then the same logic applies to Moses? Not to mention King David?

Has Pat Robertson had on his show highly regarded scholars of world religions, people like Karen Armstrong and Huston Smith, who write eloquently of the reluctant prophet Muhammad and his struggles against those in his time who fought any alteration in the status quo? Who resisted the notions of charity and piety and threatened the lives of those who converted to Islam, thus forcing them into a defensive posture?

Of course they haven't. Hate and fear sell, they fill the sanctuaries and line the pockets of those with books to market. We have enemies, the Falwells of this world preach. We do, of course. Knowing exactly who they are can take some work.

Even a cursory study of Islam and the Qur'an will reveal a religion tolerant of other faiths, with a desire to serve God and one another with kindness and brotherhood. Like the Bible, it can be twisted to justify hate, and likewise it can be misconstrued by taking parts of it out of context.

I'm not an expert on Islam, but I'm curious and I read a bit. I understand enough to know that some followers of Muhammad have committed many acts of violence in the name of Islam. I understand enough to know that they are distorting a peaceful faith, and I suspect they're doing it on purpose.

"See that none of you repays evil for evil," the apostle Paul wrote to the Thessalonians, "but always seek to do good to one another, and to all." Or maybe that was Dolly. At any rate, these are words that resonate with my Christian soul, and I can only hope my fellow believers look at them from time to time. For the Bible, like the Qur'an, is not just for thumping. Sometimes you have to read it.

All of it.

The Best Christmas Ever

I'm a Christmas Eve shopper, one of those desperate men you'll see in the mall, darting in and out of stores with a panicked expression, arms full of bags containing things no one could possibly want. I hate crowds and I hate shopping, so logically I delay it until it can be as miserable an experience as possible.

This leads to errors in judgment, of course. These make great stories for my family. My wife has probably forgotten the diamond studs, new bathrobe, and stereo system I've given her in the past, but she'll never forget the year I bought her a lovely sweater from apparently the Extremely Obese Ladies rack (the tag said "medium;" I just thought it was supposed to be big).

It was after one of these last-minute excursions, walking through the parking lot at Alderwood Mall on Christmas Eve 1990, when I noticed something in the air. It was cold and there were dark clouds in the sky, and I was in the process of trying to remember which car I had driven to the mall when a snowflake landed on my shoulder.

Snow is part of our Christmas liturgy. Scrooge shuffles through it and George Bailey runs through it, screaming for someone to recognize him. It's Currier and Ives and Budweiser commercials. As a teenager I used to crawl on the roof of our house and stare at the sky on Christmas Eve, waiting for a sign of snow.

Considering I lived in Phoenix at the time, I had a better chance of getting hit by an asteroid, but hey. I'm a mystic at Christmas. I believe in miracles.

In 1990 I was justified. I opened my eyes Christmas morning and looked upward through the blinds on the window and saw snow. Lots of it, just streaming down. After all these years of waiting, it felt suddenly strange, almost an aberration. There were several inches on the ground when we got up, and it snowed all day long.

(If you don't remember this White Christmas, I should note that it tends to snow in my neighborhood more than others. Seriously. You can ask my neighbors. Sometimes it only snows at my house. This is because we are God's Favorites.)

Snow on Christmas seemed an appropriate ending to a good year for us. It was a happy, affluent time, with my business going well, my wife's career blossoming, my daughter in kindergarten, and my 10-month-old son wandering around the house, finding all sorts of things and putting them in his mouth. I sometimes think of it as The Best Christmas Ever. And sometimes I wonder about that.

Seven years earlier, it was a different story. My wife and I had just moved to Seattle, and we lived in a one-bedroom apartment on Capitol Hill with no furniture except for a bed and a TV. We were cold all the time. We had no phone.

We also had no money, and it looked like a bleak Christmas. On Christmas Eve I walked up and down Broadway, wondering what I could get her for the few dollars I had. After I settled on a book I'd found for half price, I came back to our apartment and she was gone. An hour or so later, the intercom buzzed. I went outside and there she stood, next to our car...which had a Christmas tree strapped to the roof.

She'd found this tree for a dollar. It wasn't a pathetic Charlie Brown one, either; it was lush and full. We set it up in our empty living room and decorated it with the few ornaments we had. It was our first Christmas together, and we knew there would be others. We listened to Christmas music on the radio and danced around our tree, waiting for the future to happen.

So now I wonder about the best Christmas ever. We could fit that first apartment in our basement now, and there are dozens of ornaments and lots of furniture and, at last count, eight phones. There are packages under the tree. I wouldn't want to go back to 1983. But still.

"Somehow Tim gets thoughtful sitting by himself so much, and thinks the strangest things you ever heard. He told me, coming home, that he hoped the people saw him in the church, because he was a cripple, and it might be pleasant for them to remember upon Christmas Day, who made lame beggars walk, and blind men see."

There is something about the memory of two people, alone and poor in a strange city, that makes me think we somehow touched the soul of Christmas that year. It makes me think of a manger. It makes me think of waiting for miracles.

It'll probably rain this Christmas. It'll still be Christmas. George Bailey will get his life back and Clarence will get his wings. The

Grinch's small heart will grow three sizes. And Tiny Tim will not die.

And I will be reminded that miracles do happen, and are worth waiting for. That family is more important than furniture. That hope abounds in the human heart, that service to others is our greatest calling, that peace is worth praying for, and that, through half-closed eyes, the rain can sort of look like snow.

Teach Your Children Well

There are a million stories in the naked city, the saying goes. Or maybe it's a thousand stories in the big city. Or a million naked people, something. You know what I mean.

There were 30,000 stories in Olympia last week. Stories of sacrifice and love and commitment, I'm sure. Stories of depression and burn-out. Stories about lost children and found hope. Stories of teachers.

Public school teachers and supporters from all over Washington converged on the state capitol, reminding our legislature and governor that promises matter. The voters promised smaller classes and more money, and 30,000 gathered to remind us all that we're supposed to keep our promises.

Budgets are good things, of course; they teach us to prioritize. We learn to pay the mortgage and skip the steak, do the important stuff and trim the fat when the times are lean. Living within our means is good policy, privately and publicly. And for many of us, at different points in our lives, we've understood that in the uncertain arena of choices one thing goes without saying: First, provide for the children. I learned all this from my parents, and I also learned it from my teacher. Most of us have favorite teacher stories. This is mine.

My earliest memory of Dick Kemper was the first day of school in 1973. He was in the front of the room, mildly chewing out Tammy Evans for dropping his geometry class. He was trying to point out that she was making a mistake, and he was using a little sarcasm. Tammy probably wasn't helping her case by wearing a red halter top and blue jean shorts that were cut off fairly high up; Dick believed that you came to school to learn, not to be distracting (how do I remember what she was wearing? I was 15. I took notes. Trust me).

He was 38. I remember this because someone asked his age and he turned it into a puzzle we had to calculate, and I blurted out the answer immediately (I cheated, actually; don't tell). He thought I might have something on the ball, so he paid attention.

Or maybe it was just that I laughed at his jokes, which were mostly dumb puns about geometry terms. I can't remember any of them now, and very little of basic geometry, but 30 years later Dick Kemper remains my friend and advisor.

He told me stories about his days in college and in the service. He discussed books and theater with me as if I were an adult. He occasionally paid me to do odd jobs around his house. When my sister and several friends were in a bad car accident, he took me out for donuts and calmed me down. He steered me through three years of high school, and at the end he wrote letters of recommendation and helped me pick my college courses.

The night of graduation, he stood at the bottom of the steps of the stage and shook our hands as we went to receive our diplomas. I can see it now in my mind's eye, and somehow my life tumbles out from that moment like Dr. Seuss's "Oh, The Places You'll Go!" I can see college and marriage, mortgages and all sorts of mistakes, children and jobs and successes and disappointments, all of them jumbled and bright and dark and uplifting and frightening, and all of them cascading back to that moment, when my teacher shook my hand and told me congratulations, I'd done a good job, and it was now my turn.

Many of you have similar stories. I assume Gov. Locke does too, some teacher in his past who made a difference, provided guidance and support and changed his life. I'd hope he thinks of this in the coming weeks, as he and the legislature try to hammer out a tough budget in a tough time. I would caution him that teachers linger in our souls long after school is over, and the ghosts of those who taught us well can have a profound influence.

For I've learned, over the years, that most things change but some don't. I love my parents for instilling in me values and life lessons, for not murdering me when I was a teenager, and for always being there. I love and admire my brother and sister, for whom blood is thicker than anything. I love and cherish my old friends for the comfort they provide when I'm blue and for their understanding when I've had too many glasses of wine. All of these people are important, but I'm long past trying to impress them.

I'm 44 years old, though, and it occurs to me that whatever I've done with my life, whatever accomplishments and successes I've experienced, whatever I've tried and failed at and tried again, the thought has never been far from my mind:

I wonder if Mr. Kemper is proud of me.

The Civics Lesson

Brian Leach had a funny look on his face. It was a mixture of frustration, confusion, and concern, and it might have been hilarious had I not been certain I was wearing the exact same expression.

Along with 30 of his classmates from Jerry Morris' American Government class at Kamiak, Brian was competing in the state finals of "We the People...The Citizen and the Constitution." Ten schools were in attendance, each broken up into six teams of four or five students, each studying a variety of questions on a certain part of the Constitution and Bill of Rights. They prepared four-minute speeches for each of the (pre-selected) broad questions they might be asked, after which they answered questions from a panel of adjudicators (attorneys, judges, educators, legislators, etc.)

I was there in an unofficial capacity as an observer, and at Mr. Morris' request in an official capacity as a warm body, another adult in case, I suppose, a fistfight broke out in a heated discussion about separation of powers or the Dred Scott case. I was of absolutely no use, actually, except to smile at a particularly skilled answer or hold my head in my hands at a hard question. I mostly smiled.

I couldn't be objective. I remember many of these students from when they were in grade school, and watching them, poised and confident, elaborate on concepts so crucial to our republic was a great experience. Getting up at 4 in the morning and driving to

Olympia in the pouring rain is fairly low on the list of things I really enjoy, but this was worth it.

I saw scholarship, industry, and even some passion. I saw exquisite teamwork and some shining moments when one of them would take the ball and run with it. I saw them listen, and reason, and speak with the authority of someone who knows the subject. And I saw hope, a lot of hope.

There are constants in the history of human civilization, things we've always done and said, traits that define us as human beings. One of these is the moment that every generation has when it assesses its accomplishments and its values, and then looks at the next generation coming up and thinks that the world is in big, big trouble.

Our kids can't do simple math, we're told, or read or spell (OK, this last one might be true, but judging from my emails it's not just them). They can't find Afghanistan on a map, or Iraq or even New York. They're aimless, ambitionless, indulgent, and their music is way too loud.

It doesn't matter how much truth there is to any of this, in any given year or decade. The fact is the same thing was said about me and my contemporaries, and you and yours. This is the last gasp of youth, trying to ignore the bald spots and gum disease and hips from hell. "At least we know something about the Constitution of this country," we sneer, and, you know, we don't. Not like they do. I went to Olympia and I saw.

Brian Leach is a smart guy. He took a question on judicial review that he couldn't have prepared for, one even the questioner admitted was very difficult, a question more suited (it seemed to me) for a first-year law student. He asked for some clarification and then dove in, showing his knowledge of the situation and the issue, all of this remarkable because, as he said later, "I was answering a question that I didn't know the answer to."

I could have told him that this happens all the time in life. You just work with what you have and do your best. Unless, of course, your wife asks your opinion on her appearance, in which case your best bet is to fake a seizure. But he'll learn.

Jerry Morris should be proud of this group. So should their parents. I was, and never more so than toward the end of the morning. The question was, to paraphrase, "How can American citizens best stay informed of the issues facing their government, and hold their representatives accountable?"

My mind raced. The wide dissemination of information on the Internet. Newspapers and magazines. C-SPAN. By reading and listening, I wanted to shout. And here was the answer, echoed by every member of the team in one way or the other:

"The best way to stay informed about our government is to participate in it."

Why didn't I think of that? Because I don't have Mr. Morris reminding me every day. Because my copy of the Constitution gathers dust on a shelf, instead of being open on my desk. Because the torch is always being passed, because I'm not 18 anymore, and because I've forgotten what it was like to see a country not full of things that are broken, but of things just waiting to be fixed.

Chicken Soup For The Soul

"It's business, not personal," was the motto of the Corleone family in "The Godfather." It was a rationalization for doing bad things. It seemed to keep them content and guilt free.

Michael Corleone, the youngest son, disagreed. "It's ALL personal," he said. I know what he means.

I sit in my car on Mukilteo Speedway. I try to avoid it when I can, and sometimes I just forget and then it's too late. I'm stuck, watching as the road is torn up. Men and women in orange vests stand in front of me with a sign that says "Stop," and then after a while it says "Slow" and they wave me on. They keep waving, as if I were too stupid to understand it's time to go. I think they do that to make me feel like a fool. I think they're tearing up the road just to make me late. It's all personal.

A woman in the left turn lane in front of me bends over to check something on the passenger seat. The light turns green. She doesn't notice. I don't honk. I'm not a honker. Eventually she sits up and sees the situation and goes, but first she looks in the rearview mirror and offers me a gesture. It's not a nice gesture. You know the gesture. She's irritated at me not because of anything I did, but because of what she suspects I'm thinking. She takes it personally.

I stand in line at the grocery store. When they ask for my store card, I hand it over. "Are you going to write in the paper about these cards?" the checker asks. I ask if people are mad about the cards. She rolls her eyes. Oh, yeah. They take it personally.

I wake up in the middle of the night and grab a book from the shelf to read. It's a random choice. It's "Slaughterhouse-5" by Kurt Vonnegut. I've read it before. "Slaughterhouse-5" is the story of Billy Pilgrim, who becomes unstuck in time. It's also a fictionalized account of Vonnegut's experiences in World War II.

Kurt Vonnegut is 80 years old now, and he's angry about the impending war in Iraq. He takes it very personally. "I'm mad about being old, and I'm mad about being an American," he said in a recent interview. Harsh words. He's a famous pacifist, of course. He believes World War II was a just war, but he hasn't been crazy about wars since then. So it goes.

I'm standing in line at the grocery store to buy chicken and vegetables. The chicken is on sale. I buy two big ones, and a leek, a turnip, an onion, and some carrots. The turnip always throws the checkers. "This is..." they say, holding it up. I'm guessing they don't see a lot of turnips. I make a joke about it. I'm a jokester. I don't mention Iraq.

Lots of people are mad about the war coming up. They think it's un-American to attack first. They think it's all about oil, or Bush's dad.

Lots of people are mad about people who are mad about the war. They argue that Saddam Hussein is evil, and will get serious weapons and use them on us unless we stop him. They talk about U.N. resolutions and gassed Kurds and terrorist camps.

This is a healthy debate, I suppose, but I only watch now. I don't argue with anyone. War is often about inertia, and this one is, too. We've got 100,000 American troops sitting on Iraq's border, and they're not going to turn around. We can hope that they will, that a miracle will happen and Saddam will disclose his hidden weapons and then go away, but we know.

As I say, I think it's healthy to advocate this action by writing letters to the editor, etc. I think it's healthy to protest, to hold up signs at street corners and march. These are the tools of democrats, free speech and free assembly.

We are governed with our consent, though, and we've given it by proxy. Our representatives in Congress have given the president authority to wage war now, so war we'll get. It wasn't a particularly close vote. Terrorism had struck home. There was an election coming up. Other things. So it goes.

I'm making chicken soup. I do that when I'm worried or upset. Toss some chicken and vegetables into a stock pot, and a few hours later you have terrific soup.

I'm worried because I take it all personally. I look outside at my little corner of the world and wonder what it will look like next year. Maybe the same. Maybe it'll be a brief, efficient little war that will bring freedom to the Iraqi citizens and end a threat. Maybe not. I know nothing about the future.

But we've still gotta eat, so I make soup. Partly for that reason, and partly because it gives me pleasure, and partly because at this moment I can't think of anything else to do.

The Right Stuff

Like many of you, I have stuff around the house I never use. A skill saw. A power drill. A thesaurus. A vacuum cleaner.

Then there are books. I have college textbooks that I didn't read when I was in college. I have the collected works of Herman Hesse, purchased when people were rediscovering Hesse. I never got around to reading them, but they're here somewhere.

And there are redundancies. Three computers, plus remnants of a couple of more in the basement. Four TVs. Lots of phones. Coaxial cables and Y-connectors and several thousand (my estimate) unpaired socks. Some stuffed animals no one has quite given up on yet. Dozens of videotapes. Several hundred screwdrivers, all missing. And no globe.

How can I have grown so old and yet not own a globe? I love globes. In libraries or my kids' classrooms, I always go for the globe.

It's mysterious, this attraction. It's become an element of a personal sacrament, a piece of matter that transforms me. I spin it and caress it and study it. I compare continents and trace distances from my home to other places, but mostly I look, on this sphere, for corners.

These are the unknown places, the last mysteries on a small planet. Antarctica. Nepal. Micronesia. Unknown just to me;

there is no undiscovered country anymore, but there are places, far-flung and remote, that stir my soul.

I want to see Point Barrow. I want to stand on cliffs in northern Scotland and experience the Aurora Borealis. Or south, to Cape Horn and watch penguins scamper on the shores of South America, under craggy mountains at the end of the earth.

These are Walter Mitty dreams, of course. I'm a middle-aged, overweight man with poor eyesight and back problems. The only exploring I'm likely to do is on the highways of America or in the organic food section of the supermarket.

I had an email from a resident of Kuwait recently, a reaction to a column I wrote in another publication that got posted on the Web. "It must be easy to be sarcastic," she wrote, "living in such a safe place." Yes. It is. I do.

This is what I've been thinking about this past week, watching the Columbia news and memorials. Questions have been raised about why we grieve so strongly for these seven astronauts, when others who serve us die in the line of duty and their passing goes largely unnoticed by the nation. This is good to acknowledge, I think; the lives of soldiers killed in a helicopter crash or cops cut down on the job are as worthy of national mourning.

There is something different, though, about these seven. Their deaths have reminded us of their resumes, and of the types of people we send into space. Men and women, Israeli and African-American, Christian and Hindu -- their differences are overshadowed by their remarkable journeys that led them to Columbia.

We've gotten complacent, we're told, about the dangers of "slipping the surly bonds of earth." We've also forgotten, I think, that there is such a thing as excellence, and that there are superior people, perhaps not bred as much as formed by their desire to dream and commitment to pursue those dreams.

My son turned 13 today, as I write, nearly six feet tall and 160 pounds, a man in an earlier era, ready for war or exploration. He lives in a safe place and time, though, relatively speaking. I wish I had given him a globe for his birthday. I wish I could relate the awe I felt, much younger than he, when the rockets first went up. We watched them then, and drew pictures in school of space walks and capsules. In 1981, when I was 22, a buddy and I stayed up all night so we could see the launch of the first space shuttle and relive a little of our childhood.

The American space program sprang out of the shock of Sputnik, an affront to a nation that had begun to believe it could do anything. It was articulated at Rice University in 1962 by John Kennedy, who said we chose to go to the moon "Not because it is easy, but because it is hard."

This was an appeal to nationalism, of course, pure Cold War politics, but filtered through the sensibilities of a man who'd been a sickly child, reared on stories of King Arthur and knights. It appealed more to our awareness of what human begins have always done, searching for the unknown because it was there.

"Here There Be Dragons" was written on the ancient maps for places yet to be explored, and filled with assumed danger. It was a warning to the cautious, and a beacon to the adventurous.

This is who these seven were, then, and why I've wiped away tears this week, grieving for people I didn't know. It's a sorrow based on young lives lost and children left behind, and sacrifice that knew the risks. It's a personal sorrow, for those who explore the unknown on my behalf. It's a sorrow that marks the vagaries of nature, the uncertainty of life, and the courage and passion of those who would seek out dragons, last seen streaking across a bright blue Texas sky.

What Have I Got To Lose? (don't answer)

We've all seen the charts. We've heard about Body Mass Index. Sometimes our clothes inexplicably shrink. And suddenly we wonder, after all these years, if we're fat.

A few years ago, Dave Barry came up with a good method of answering the question, something you can do in the privacy of your own home. "Stand up straight," he wrote, "suck in your gut, and look out the window. If you live in America, you're fat."

I should note for the record that I am a full-blooded, born-in-the-USA, Mayflower-rooted American. In case my picture up there is misleading. You can do amazing things with the proper lighting.

This is old news. Americans have gotten fatter decade by decade, we read, but then we can just look out the window. And we start 'em young: Obesity in our kids is now called an epidemic.

The reasons are pretty clear, too: Fast food, larger portions, sugary cereal and soda, and a 20-year fascination with "low-fat" food that turned out to be loaded with all sorts of nasty stuff to make it taste good.

Add into this mix an increasingly sedentary population, sitting in front of TVs or computers, and even with the popularity of gyms and our skinny icons of fashion and celebrity, America is waddling. And it ain't pretty.

I know all about this. As I say, a true-blue American here. Thirteen years ago, I ran four miles every morning and weighed 155 pounds. My mom worried that I was too thin.

Shortly after that, I started a business, parked my butt in an ergonomically designed chair in front of a computer, and a couple of years later I noticed that my neighbor started greeting me by saying, "How you doing, big guy?" Big guy. Mom had new reasons to worry.

Not an untypical American story, or particularly interesting. And I've adjusted all right. I don't care to have my picture taken or spend a lot of time in front of a full-length mirror, but I'm fairly comfortable with my body.

Except I'm not. Comfortable, that is. I'm getting back problems and neck problems. Walking uphill isn't as fun as it used to be. And ten years down the road things could get interesting, just statistically speaking. Joint problems. Heart disease. And that old reliable, diabetes. What's a fat guy to do?

I know, I know. And I've done it on a couple of occasions for a short time. I've never had any use for fad diets or weight loss centers. Just increase the fruits and vegetables, shy away from animal fats, eat less than necessary to maintain my weight, and walk briskly 45-60 minutes a day; this has always worked, and the weight has always come off. And come back, of course, when I stop.

"Nothing would be more tiresome than eating and drinking," said Voltaire, "if God had not made them a pleasure as well as a necessity." And in these tense days, with Orange Alerts and wars and rumors of wars, food can be comfort as well as sustenance.

Eating is communal, too, and potlucks and pancake breakfasts can be great fun. I'm a big believer in the pleasure of good food; show me a plate of chicken fried steak, corn on the cob and mashed potatoes with gravy and I will call it happiness, pure and simple.

But there can be too much of a good thing, and sometimes big guys have a tendency to drop dead in their 50s. And where would that leave you? Trust me, if I'm gone Larry Simoneaux will be out of control. Seriously.

Then there's the patriotic aspect. How can America be a beacon of hope for the world if no more than two of us can fit in an elevator at the same time? To distort Barry Goldwater something awful, moderation in the defense of freedom is no vice. It's my duty as an American to set an example. And a fat man shall lead them...

So I start this week. I've got a sensible plan. I've got a goal. I'm not going to do anything crazy, but by June I expect to be healthier and slimmer, and if I become a babe magnet then, hey, sometimes you gotta sacrifice.

Support in this noble endeavor is crucial, of course, so I've told some people. I've discussed it with my wife and kids, who seem to think it's about time.

And I've just told about 50,000 of you, too. This is my secret weapon, actually, my responsibility to my fellow citizens, because we're all Americans here and I owe it to you, and if I don't drop some weight then the terrorists will have won. You can count on me. My only regret is that I have but 75 pounds to shed for my country.

OK, maybe 80. Depends.

Angels Among Us

Years ago my son drew me a picture, one of those innocent gestures on the part of a child guaranteed to cause permanent psychological damage to his parents.

It was a picture of me in my office downstairs, sitting in front of the computer, and he was on the other side of the door, knocking. Many strange symbols were drawn coming out of my mouth, and none of them looked polite.

This is a downside to working at home with small children in the house. There is no work ethic for children, no awareness of bills that need to be paid or deadlines that need to be met. They want daddy, and they know where to find him. If you work in an office downtown and have small children at home, I can assure you the only reason they haven't shown up at your place of business yet is that they haven't learned how to call a cab.

I was reminded of the picture last week, when my son knocked on my door again. It was at the end of the day and I was tying up loose ends, writing emails and sending files. He sounded excited.

"Dad? Can you come see something? It's really important."

"Is it so important that it can't wait 20 minutes? Because that's when I'll be up."

"Oh, all right." Sound of receding footsteps, slowing trudging back up the stairs.

Immediately I knew what a fool I was. Here I'd been moping around for weeks, walking by my daughter's bedroom knowing that in six months she'll be going away to college and it'll be empty for the first time in 15 years, and I couldn't find five minutes for my son? Did I really think he'd be 13 forever, wanting to share his excitement and discoveries?

This is what they don't tell you in the parenting books, that for all the various stages of ambulation and developmental milestones, there will come a time when, oddly enough, the children grow up.

What I find myself missing now are the little things, the trivial moments that seem mundane and slide by without notice. It's easy to remember the trips to Disneyland and the first day of school, the end of diapers and the beginning of reading. Digging through old videos the other day, though, I came across our complete collection of Winnie the Pooh episodes and wondered when we watched them last. I still know the theme song by heart. I'm singing it right now. "He's warm and he's fuzzy/I love him because he's/Our Pooh bear, Winnie the Pooh Bear..."

And last week, I wondered how long it'd been since I sat in the living room with my children and heard that familiar piano music, and watched Mr. Rogers walk through that same door. They'd be entranced but so would I, sitting in front of the TV and secretly hoping this was the one when he goes to the peanut butter factory. He was my neighbor, too.

He was the best kind of neighbor, the kind who lends you a lawnmower and demonstrates the right way to plant a flower bed. He was a soothing, comforting voice among the Power

Rangers and Mutant Turtles on television, but he was an asset to us, also.

When my son was 5, he asked me, "What is heaven?" I wasn't surprised at the question; he'd been in Sunday School all his life. I was curious, though, so I said, "Umm...why do you ask, John?" He stared out the window, thinking. "Because I don't know," he said.

What a dumb grownup thing for me to say. What a perfectly natural question for him to ask. And what an opportunity Mr. Rogers would have had to show me how to do better. "Heaven can be a SCARY idea sometimes, can't it?" he'd say, and off they'd go. I learned there are lots of worse things than wondering, "What Would Mr. Rogers Do?" when it came to my children.

On Mr. Rogers' website, there is advice for parents to help their children deal with the news of his death. What about me? I wondered, but I know what he would say. Our job is to take care of the children, to help them feel safe, to answer their questions, to show them that they are loved. There is no greater calling, he believed. I believe it, too.

I don't know what heaven is. I don't know the dimensions or the location. I don't know the criteria for admission and I don't know if I'm on a list. I haven't a clue about the food situation.

But I'm aware of heaven, as surely as my children are aware that I'm downstairs in my office. I like to believe that it's a place of pure peace and joy, free from hate and war. And I'd like to believe that it's a place for children, where their questions are always answered and their souls are nurtured, where they're safe at last and forever, and where they are now watched over for eternity by an angel in a cardigan sweater.

Springtime For Somebody, Somewhere

I got to know my neighbors better the other day. This is a good thing, of course; it helps create a sense of community and security. What was nice about it was that I didn't even have to, you know, go outside or anything.

I was on the Internet, searching through various databases from the 2000 census of my neighborhood (do I have a life or what?). There's a ton of information there, most of it incredibly boring, but it provided a little snapshot of the three or four blocks that make up my home.

The first fact that jumped out at me was that my neighborhood is white. This wasn't a surprise, although 40 years after "I have a dream" it seems segregation is alive and well, if not codified. Over 70% of us are white, with another 12% or so Asian. The rest breaks down into miniscule percentages of Hispanics, Pacific Islanders, etc. Only 1.5% are black.

That percentage increases dramatically if you just take my house and the one next door, since my neighbor is African-American. We've never discussed demographics. Actually, we rarely talk, since he works a swing shift, although we did have a nice chat two years ago right after the earthquake. We were both at home and rushed outside, and we had what was possibly the dumbest conversation ever after a 7-plus shaker:

HIM: Did you feel that?

ME: Yeah. Did you?

Probably the most striking piece of information from the census was that this is a fairly young neighborhood. The largest percentage of the population falls between 30 and 50 years of age, with the median age being about 34. Staying away from such technical terms as "median," though, looking through all this data I could extrapolate a typical person on my block. He's male, 44, married with two children, a homeowner with a passion for Gene Hackman movies and baseball. He might write a column. This is just off the top of my head, of course.

This was a census, not a poll, so there was nothing about what my neighbors are thinking. And back in 2000, pre-hanging chad, pre-recession, pre-9-11, it probably wouldn't have been all that interesting.

I have no idea what my neighbors think about the upcoming war in Iraq. I'd guess they're pretty representative of the rest of the country. That is, we're split. Looking at recent figures, you could say that a slim majority of Americans favors our intervention. You could also say that a larger majority either does not or favors it only with U.N. backing. These are just numbers, though; you can pretty much make them work anyway you want. And when the battle begins, probably sometime next week, the favorable numbers will go way up. Americans rally, at least in the beginning.

Eighteen months ago, I watched Jeff Greenfield on CNN. He was standing on a rooftop in New York City, overlooking a drastically changed landscape, and he told us that from now on our world would be different. Yes, and no. Travel is more complicated. We think more about who we are and why people would hate us. We've learned some new terms. New Yorkers are still dealing with trauma.

But my street is the same. Warm weather has forced an early spring, and everything is blossoming. People still jog and take walks. People still fill up their cars, even at $1.80 a gallon. Children still walk to school.

War is different to a neighborhood of boomers and X-ers. We weren't around in World War II, with service stars in the windows and Victory Gardens and blackouts. And our memories of Vietnam are of polarization, of deferments and of mothers hiding their sons in the trunks of their cars for the trip to Canada. Later, we unified casually behind relatively painless conflicts: Grenada, Panama, Kuwait, Haiti, Bosnia. War has become remote; we can always just switch the channel.

Friends, loved ones, and neighbors have been shipping out, of course. There's plenty of concern and fear in our neighborhoods. Demographically speaking, though, for most of us Gulf War II will be a mini-series. We'll gather around the set and marvel at the sophistication of our technology. We'll await news of Saddam's retreat or death. We'll hope for dancing, not fighting, in the streets of Baghdad. And it will still be springtime here, and we'll still be safe.

When the bombing starts, we might not be thinking about numbers. Demographics show that a majority of the population of Iraq is under the age of 15. They're not our enemies, of course, and we'll try everything we can to avoid collateral damage. But we'll be attacking a country of children. It's nice that we can turn off the TV.

We'll go outside then, and enjoy our early spring. Maybe a walk at the end of the day to clear our minds. For even after 9/11 and anthrax, and nuclear threats from North Korea and Iran, we can still feel safe in our neighborhoods far away from war. The battle will rage but the bombs will be distant, and if we hear a sudden noise overhead we'll know it's only a flock of birds, returning home in the spring after a short and mild winter.

Real Men Don't Floss

In these tense times, I thought a little humor might help take your minds off current events. So here's one of my favorite jokes:

A man walks into a dentist's office.

Oh, man, that always makes me laugh. I'll wait until you catch your breath. Don't you feel better?

I know I'm perpetuating a stereotype here, and that there are plenty of men out there who visit the dentist regularly, change their underwear daily, etc. Statistically speaking, though, a grown man is as likely to see a dentist of his own volition as he is to volunteer to see a Meg Ryan movie.

Part of this is our natural love of redundancy. After all, aren't we blessed with two eyes, two ears, two kidneys, two livers, etc.? If the Good Lord saw fit to give us 32 teeth, they must be there for back-up purposes. How many teeth does it take to drink a beer? How many does it take to eat a pretzel? (Answer: Four, although it can be done with three.)

There's also a genetic reason, part of our pioneer make-up that urges us to ignore trifling matters such a teeth. Did Davy Crockett, King of the Wild Frontier, worry about cavities? I think not. He probably took a shot of rotgut liquor and then went off to the Alamo to fight alongside John Wayne and David Bowie. This was a man, remember, who killed hisself a bear when he was only three (Note: He probably did not bite the bear). What's a little pain?

Ah. Well. "A little pain" can sometimes take on the significance of "a little bit pregnant." A couple of weeks ago, I found myself on a Saturday night, when all the dental professionals were safely tucked away in bed, visions of sugarless plums dancing through their heads, pondering the meaning of life and why a molar had decided to turn on me when I had done nothing to it. I decided it was time to find a dentist.

I picked Gail Kautzman, D.D.S., because her name was in my insurance directory and her office was just north of the Speedway on Highway 99, close enough to my house that I could crawl there, which seemed a possibility. I spoke with Mary on the phone, a very kind woman who apparently serves as part office manager and part tooth counselor. I got in the same day.

Dr. Kautman's dental assistant, Cynthia, was a young woman who was also kind and reassuring. She took a quick x-ray, expressed her sympathy for my pain, and asked me when I'd last seen a dentist. I decided to make a game out of it.

"What year were you born, Cynthia?"

"1983."

"Umm...forget it."

Gail Kautzman turned out to be the perfect dentist for me, professional and friendly with a nice sense of humor. Aside from casually mentioning that, in her opinion, a visit every six months was preferable to every couple of decades, and aside from sticking a needle into the roof of my mouth, which I thought was kind of rude, she went about easing my pain.

This involved, as it turned out, removing the offending molar, along with the wisdom tooth next to it. This was all right with me, although I could hardly have said no. Because I couldn't say anything by that time; my tongue seemed to have disappeared, and the only sound I was capable of making was "waasdawek." She took this for consent.

Going to the dentist after a long time away is like getting the oil changed in your car after three years. You'll get new oil, but the mechanic is likely to find a whole list of things that need to be fixed. After a deep cleaning, two of my front lower teeth seemed to be less than lively. It turns out that all the stuff that had accumulated on them, 20 years worth of plaque, calculus, bits of potato chips, etc., had sort of a stabilizing effect, and once removed the teeth became a little tentative. "Try not to sneeze," Dr. Kautzman said helpfully.

They also were discolored, and now they hurt, so a day later I was back in the chair, discovering the miracles of modern dentistry. She pulled the teeth, showed them to me (they looked like something dug up in Tanzania by the Leakey Foundation), went away for a while (during which time I assume she took them around to show the other dentists in the building, posted pictures of them on the Internet, etc.), and came back with two gleaming white teeth, which she proceeded to GLUE BACK IN MY MOUTH (kids, get your parents' permission first).

So, thanks to Dr. Kautzman and her staff, I now have clean teeth and no pain, and I've learned it's never too late to visit your dentist. I've learned not to take my teeth for granted. And I've come to appreciate Meg Ryan a little more. I think she's a darn fine actress. And she's got a great smile.

Truth, Justice, and the American Way. Or Else.

How come Superman never got arrested?

See, I think if you're honest with yourself, you have to admit Superman did some highly questionable things. He was forever tossing stuff into outer space. If he even once obeyed the speed limit, it's news to me. He changed clothes in public places. He was constantly arresting crooks on his own volition with no Miranda recitation, and often he just dropped them off at prison without benefit of trial or conviction. Superman should have had a rap sheet a mile long.

(Okay, some of you are going to be tempted to write to inform me that, in fact, Superman WAS arrested, more than once, and can document this with dates and issues. Please. Let me have my one lousy metaphor.)

It's a rhetorical question. We all know the answer. Superman was never arrested because nobody could.

Superman was a good guy, of course. And we're good guys, too. U.S. history is littered with mistakes, errors of judgment, blunders and just plain wrong moves, but our heart is in the right place. And there are convincing arguments for attacking Iraq, sound reasoning and even some legal cover. But we're bombing Baghdad now for one very distinct (if ethically suspect) reason: Nobody can stop us.

This is the legacy of Lech Walesa, of the fall of the Berlin wall and a Russian woman wagging her finger at a young soldier in a tank on the streets of Moscow. The end of the Cold War left us with a peace dividend of power, unchecked and unbalanced. It's no surprise that much of the world fears us more the Saddam Hussein. Saddam is a pipsqueak, a trifle, a third-rate Lex Luther with a few grams of kryptonite socked away in a bunker. We are the Man of Steel and we make the rules.

We're not invulnerable. We can be hurt; we have been and probably will be again. And even if our power is unchecked, our leaders aren't. The commander in chief of our armed forces derives his authority not by coup or primogeniture, but by the consent of the governed, elected by a majority of American voters.

Okay, maybe that's not a good example in this case. But you get my point.

We spent over a decade hiding behind a mild-mannered secret identity, posing as a peaceful world leader, marshaling support, forming coalitions, speaking softly and keeping the stick in storage. We gently flexed in our own hemisphere a bit and led the rest of the world when it was necessary, but we kept the glasses on and the cape hidden.

Now the world understands, and they don't like it. Our rationale for war is irrelevant; few outside this country accept it, and we don't care anyway. A couple of weeks ago President Bush asked for cards on the table, and then decided he wasn't interested. War is in our self-interest, he says, and self-interest beats any hand when you're the biggest on the block. America has come out of the phone booth.

I suspect this is what we'll be dealing with from now on, regardless of the results of the Iraq conflict. We can establish a democratic Iraq, help create a Palestinian state, bolster the world economy, mediate disputes, make up with France and Germany, and kiss all the babies we want. The world will remember, and be suspicious. And it will probably be worse than that.

The tricky thing about using the end to justify the means, as in this case, is that you'd better be sure you know what the end will be. The world will be a better and safer place without Saddam Hussein; even the French know this. But even the rosiest scenario leaves a world community that will be wary of American power and intent, and that's just our allies.

I can only hope for the best. I can only wish our troops well, be proud of the attempts they make to spare innocent lives, and grieve with the families who will suffer loss.

I will also think about terrorism, and about how liberation can look a lot like occupation, depending on your politics. And I'll stand outside and look to the northwest, and think about Kim Jong iI. Preemptive war sets an uncomfortable precedent, and the best way to bring a big guy down has always been to strike first.

I think the dictator of North Korea is as loony a leader as the world has these days. I also know that a frightened man is a dangerous man, particularly when he's armed, and I have a feeling Kim Jong iI is scared now. Me, too.

Lost and Found

We never hear about good news in the media, or at least we like to think. It's there, of course. "If it bleeds, it leads" is a journalistic cliché, but happy stories are out there. Some are harder to find than others.

Jessica Lynch is one. The private from West Virginia, who left an impoverished life to join the Army and maybe get an education, has a happy story that we know all about. Not only was she rescued from the Iraqi hospital, but her savior was an Iraqi citizen who found that values are absolute in war, regardless. "Mohammed" caught sight of her being slapped around by one of Saddam's thugs and risked his life, and the lives of his family, to save her. Thank God for happy stories, especially in war. Gives us some hope.

This one you probably don't know about. Last Friday morning, a seventh-grader at a private school a few miles north of Seattle fell asleep in class. I mean, conked out, head on the desk, out. He had to be shaken awake, and his teachers decided as a punishment (excuse me, "consequence") he would be placed at a desk outside in the parking lot and given make-up work to do. This apparently is a favorite strategy of theirs. No coddling at this school.

Do you remember it being a little nippy last week? I do. In fact, on that day I recall looking at the little temperature icon on my computer screen and wondering if it was ever going to break into the 40s. A brisk morning, to say the least.

Now, here's the interesting thing. This is a school for children with special needs, and this kid has a pervasive developmental disorder. This sounds like a lot of psychological mumbo-jumbo, but in fact it's a well-documented neurological condition that's been identified since well into the last century.

I happen to know something about this, actually. It's sort of fascinating. People like this have recently been studied with contrast-enhanced CT scans, and the results are striking. Their brains respond in remarkable ways to sensory stimuli.

This child, like many others with this disorder, is acutely sensitive to his environment. Sounds, temperature, touch: His brain processes input from his senses in unique ways, and he has trouble with any kind of extremes. It's just something he has to learn to deal with.

After an hour or so of shaking in the cold, unable to focus on his work, he knocked on the locked door of the school and pleaded with his teachers. He promised to do all his work if they'd let him back in where it was warm. Tough cookies. That's the consequence for the crime of falling asleep. So then he told them he'd leave the school if they didn't let him in. Slam. Click. Bye-bye.

I also know something about special education teachers. My brother, Bill, has spent more than 25 years in this field. He once told me of a boy in his class who punched him every day. At the end of the year, Bill considered it a victory that the boy was punching him a little less. They are underpaid and overworked, and they do their jobs because they care about kids, particularly damaged kids.

So I'm not going to pass judgment on these teachers in this space. You'll probably have your own opinions. I know I do.

I should also mention that this particular boy was wearing a coat, and he is 13. This is an age where we might expect to feel a little more secure about a child wandering away from supervision. But, again, this is a special kid. He has a view of the world different from yours or mine. He trusts people. He is virtually incapable of reading body language, whether it's from a Good Samaritan or a pedophile.

So his parents were a little frantic when they got the nonchalant call from the school. "Have you heard from your son?" Somehow I think the Army approached the Lynch family a little differently. The mother stayed by the phone while the father sped sound down I-5, trying not to imagine scenarios he really didn't want to imagine.

Because for every Elizabeth Smart, there are Megans and Pollys who don't make it home. It's a dangerous world, full of sinners as well as saints, and not knowing is always the worst. For the better part of an hour, a boy scoured the sidewalks for loose change to call home while his parents waited and watched.

His father found him at a gas station a few blocks from school, huddled in a phone booth. So, as I said, this is a happy story. One that will only make this paper, because the relief we all must feel at such a happy ending is a little more acute for me.

As you probably suspected, it was me searching the streets, and my son. I've grown used to the fear that comes with having children, but each time it strikes it's fresh and unsettling. And relief is an emotion fed by what might have been, so it was with sort of mixed feelings that I drove into that Chevron station to find my son, glad to see me, glad to be finally warm, and only mildly puzzled by his newfound knowledge that pennies don't work in pay phones.

Report From The Front. And Back. And Sides.

I'll say this about Robert Atkins, who died last week after a fall: He stuck to his guns. For over 30 years, he actively promoted a weight loss regimen that was widely denounced by virtually the entire medical community, including that guy who only plays a doctor on TV.

Dr. Atkins never gave up, though, bolstered by the strange notion that his plan must be good because people actually lost weight on it.

Recently, a couple of studies attempted to prove him wrong, once and for all. They followed a group of people on the Atkins plan and did periodic lab tests. And sure enough, their cholesterol levels changed. They went through the floor. People got healthier.

This was in the news about eight weeks ago. And eight weeks ago, by a remarkable coincidence, I announced in this fine publication that America was fat, and that as your representative, out of the goodness of my heart, I elected to take on the responsibility of setting an example and leading America out of the wilderness and into a pair of (metaphorical) Speedos.

For various reasons, I was looking ahead about four months, making this about the halfway point. So, you want to know how I'm doing?

Not bad. Pretty good, actually.

We talk a lot about weight loss in this country. Mostly talk. And people want to lose for different reasons. Some do it for their health, others for vanity (I did it for the money, but that's not working out so well).

There are lots of different ways to lose weight, too, including eating less and exercising more (this has been documented extensively). You can count calories, fat, carbohydrates, protein, or all of the above. Or you can just stay fat and happy. This always sounded good to me.

But, no. I had to write a column and you had to read it. Try buying ice cream in the grocery store (for my wife, I swear) feeling dozens of Mukilteo eyes on your back. Maybe I'm a little paranoid.

Like most people who find themselves forty-ish and fat, I sincerely believed that this had nothing to do with what I ate. I was pretty sure that it was due to the Fat Fairy, who late at night, when I was asleep, would sneak into my bedroom and make lipo-deposits to my obliques.

So I first had to look at the way I ate, and when I ate certain foods. Take pizza and burritos. I examined my feelings very carefully and discovered that the most likely time for me to eat pizza and burritos was when I was awake.

This was disturbing, as I am usually awake at least a quarter of the day. But I took a deep breath and swore off these foods, replacing them with roasted chicken breast and leafy green vegetables, which almost immediately put me to sleep. I was on my way.

No, I'm just kidding. I felt great and had sustained energy. I eliminated bread, potatoes, pasta, rice, and all forms of sugar from my diet, and I ate frequent small meals. I never felt hungry. I drank a lot of water because people say you should but I don't know why.

I took my protein from mostly turkey and chicken, my fat from fish and small amounts of cheese, and my carbohydrates from vegetables. I didn't drink milk or alcohol, and my caffeine intake (only tea anyway) dropped to practically nothing.

And I lost weight like crazy. Sometimes my scale would develop a sense of humor and I'd have to get a little tough ("Now, you know and I know that I didn't gain 3 pounds yesterday, so let's just try this again, shall we?"), but the pounds and inches melted away.

I read a lot about obesity. I learned about set points and metabolic resistance. It turns out that a guy who gains a lot of weight suddenly, then changes his diet and loses a lot of weight quickly has less of a metabolic problem than a food addiction problem (i.e., eats mostly foods that are consumed by your average male during your average football game).

So how am I doing? I unbuckle my pants and they fall to the floor, so I avoid doing that in public. I try on clothes a lot. I listen to my family call me "skinny" when I'm really not, but I listen anyway. I've lost at least 5 inches from around my stomach.

And eight weeks ago I said I needed to lose about 80 pounds. Not to be thin (that wouldn't do it), just to be healthier. So now it's about 40. Those will be the hard ones, and I have no illusions that they'll come off in two months. But some of them will.

I'll check in with you in another eight weeks or so. Just wanted to let you know that it's not impossible, because if I can do it, anybody can.

And the ice cream was for my wife. Seriously. Stop staring.

The Dance Lesson

The school year will be over in a few weeks, so soon it'll be yearbook time.

Let me tell you about yearbooks, you who don't know, who never cared or else are still too young to realize. Yearbooks are the most powerful force in the universe. Yearbooks resist laws of physics. They laugh at quaint ideas of time and space. Yearbooks take you back, and they take you fast. Open your yearbook with caution. Things are waiting for you there.

My high school senior yearbook is around here somewhere. I pretend to lose it sometimes, so I don't have to look at it and my kids can't find it and laugh at my hair. But it's here in my office, under stuff.

It isn't about pictures. We have pictures, baby photos and wedding albums. They can move us, but it's just reflected light captured on paper, flat and distant. Reminders. Yearbooks are alive, because people write in them. It's like opening a book to find a pressed flower or dried blood; there's DNA there, and it can shock us back in time.

We remember who wrote what, and remember exactly when. I look through my yearbook and read. Some people I still know. One I see a lot. One is dead. And so on.

And there, in a girlish script, in an ink that still seems sort of phosphorescent, Karen Parinello wrote me a note. I had a little crush on Karen, not much of anything, and we only dated once.

But she had nice things to say, and then at the end of her message she reached out 27 years into the future to grab onto my soul and shake it.

"P.S.: Thank you for teaching me how to waltz."

It had been in the spring, a fundraiser for our marching band, who were going to Philadelphia that July to take place in the bicentennial celebration. They set up in the parking lot of a mall and played music for 24 hours, as I recall; maybe less, but it went on all night. They played a waltz, and people were dancing, so I asked Karen. She said she didn't know how. I said it was easy, I'd show her.

A few months earlier, I'd auditioned for a part in our school play. I thought I had a good chance, except for that dancing thing. As the saying goes, I had two left feet and the right one wasn't so hot, either. The choreographer tried to teach me a waltz, and I heard snickering in the wings.

I came home late that night to find my mother waiting up for me, as usual. I told her my frustrations, my inadequacy and my failure. I said I was going to give up.

She put down the book she'd been reading, and she told me things only a mother knows. She recited my entire history, problems I'd encountered and overcome, solutions I'd found, answers I'd discovered. She told me what I'd done and what I might possibly do, and then she went over to the stereo and put on music, and for 40 minutes or so my mother danced with me.

The yearbook is messing with my mind again. Suddenly I'm on the outside, looking in. I stand on the street and watch through the window as they dance around the living room. He is 17 and she is 39. She has work in the morning and he has life waiting for him, but for a while she teaches him how to waltz. ONE, two three, ONE, two, three.

I got the part, and if Mom took some credit for that she never said a word. ONE, two, three.

I've told her this all before, with some of the same words. She probably thinks I'm recycling my life for publication. I am, I am. ONE, two, three.

But I'm telling it to you now, because this Sunday is Mother's Day and it's not too late. I know, I know. It's a Hallmark Holiday, and reeks of legislated emotion and forced confessions. Of course I love my mother. Why should I have to tell her every May because you say I should?

Because I don't do it enough, is why. And I don't say thank you nearly enough, either.

So, thanks, Mom. Thanks for teaching me to tie my shoes. Thanks for making my lunches. Thanks for giving me your recipes. Thanks for teaching me to love music and theater.

Thanks for making me wash the dishes and clean my room. Thanks for loving my children. Thanks for sharing your memories. Thanks for teaching me how to make tacos.

Thanks for being cold and aloof to me when I was rude and thoughtless to you. Thanks for showing me that common courtesy starts with your family, or it never starts.

Thanks for showing me all the things I could do, if only I'd remember the things I've already done.

And P.S.: Thank you for teaching me how to waltz. It was just one of many moments, but some of those are still alive, like the writing in a yearbook. We are still dancing, I am still learning to believe, you are still teaching me, and looking back at my life I'm still convinced that has made all the difference.

Becoming Moe

His name was Moe Axelrod, and he was a character. A Jewish gangster in Depression-era New York, he was cynical, sharp, a ladies man, world-weary, one-legged, and a romantic at heart.

And fictional. Moe was the creation of Clifford Odets, in his play "Awake And Sing!" Moe was first played by Luther Adler, one of the founders of the famed Group Theater in the early part of the 20th century. Fifty years or so later, I got a shot at Moe in a college production.

It was an actor's dream, a part to dive into and disappear. A Brooklyn accent with a hint of a Yiddish lilt, hair dyed jet black and a little putty augmentation for my puny nose, a pencil-thin moustache and a limp.

And a cigarette. Of course. Not only was it in the stage directions, but c'mon: This was the 1930s. Moe was a smoker.

But I wasn't. I grew up in a smoking household; my father was a serious smoker, and he had a chronic cough and that didn't sound like a whole lot of fun, so I was never interested. I had my rebellious moments as a teenager and my risky business, but smoking was never part of it.

The director was irritated with me, though. "It doesn't look real," he said about my attempts to fake smoking on stage. Listen: There are certain things you can say to a serious student actor to get his attention. You want real? I'll show you real.

So, for the sake of art, I grabbed one of our prop unfiltered (of course) Lucky Strikes, lit that baby up and inhaled deeply. Then I sat down real fast. A few more puffs and I lost my lunch.

But I managed after a while. I carried those Luckys with me and I smoked them until my light-headedness left and I was able not to gag or cough. It was a great acting tool, actually. I'd sit in the makeup room before the curtain and smoke, looking into the mirror, becoming Moe.

The play had an extended run, so I smoked for a couple of months. It was sort of sad at the end, knowing it was time to hand over my cigarettes. Almost like losing an old friend. But I knew I had to quit, so I did.

And it only took me 11 years.

I didn't want to quit. I liked smoking. The habit was starting to increase, though, and I had kids, so I impulsively threw them away one day. But I missed them.

Maybe this explains why I've flirted with them ever since. Bumming one off a smoking friend. Buying a pack spontaneously for a lonely road trip and then tossing two-thirds of it away in disgust. Smoking for a weekend and then not thinking about it for months. Sort of binge smoking. And always trying to keep it a secret.

Stressful times are the worst, of course. I've had my share of stress in the past few years, and my share of cigarettes.

I'm pretty sure I'm done with them now, though. You can never tell; smoking, some say, has a higher recidivism rate than heroin and it's easier to get. But I think my smoking days are over.

I don't mean to be an alarmist. Other than some sneezing and congestion this spring, I feel good. I have energy. I'm eating better. I have fairly good exercise endurance. In other words, it's not because I have lung cancer.

It's because my dad does.

I'm not stupid, regardless of how I look. I knew the risks, and so did he. We all have vices of some sort or the other, and we gamble with our health from time to time. I could tell you things about French fries.

It's just that they taste bad now. They taste like death, like bad decisions and irreparable mistakes. They taste like tumors.

I'm not lecturing anyone, either. Actually, I've always sort of liked smokers, in a twisted way; they wear their weakness on their sleeves. And teeth. And fingers.

And lungs. And lymph glands. And liver. In my dad's case.

It'll be easy, too. I just decided to replace one habit with another. Now, instead of smoking cigarettes, I will get a chest x-ray. Once a year. For 10 years. When I can breathe a little easier. But I'll still get them, hoping that's the only dose of radiation I will ever need.

I'm also not writing this to inform young people of the dangers of smoking. They know. Everyone knows. I guess I'm just writing to say, to those who've never taken that first puff, that it's probably not a good idea. And for a reason the anti-smoking groups won't tell you, although they should. See, it's not because it might kill you one day.

It's because you might like it.

The Prophecy

It is his favorite picture of her, he realizes suddenly one day, and then wonders why it took so long to figure that out. Maybe it's a sign of maturity, or middle-age; after years of trying to keep an open mind with shifting tastes and likes, the races are over and there are winners. This is the book, the song, the movie, the moment. This is the picture.

She is a Texan. He knows this, of course, but then anyone would, he thinks. Who else would rehearse an opera, be captured on film interpreting the music of Mozart, wearing cowboy boots?

He gives her the boots on her 28th birthday, years before the picture, his way of acknowledging who she is and also surrendering to a more powerful culture. I give up. Y'all win.

She goes home a month before their wedding, to have it out on home turf. "What does this boy do?" her father asks, and she sticks up for love. "He's an actor and a writer," she says defiantly, and the screen door slams and there are words. Not a good sign.

He meets the in-laws the day before they marry, and his bride-to-be holds onto his arm as if he's about to bolt, which he is thinking seriously about. Her mother hugs him, trusting her daughter, but daddy just says, "So this is what you brung us," and sticks out a meaty hand. To his credit, he has a slight smile. This will only hurt a little.

He finds his first trip to Texas disorienting, disturbing. It's flat, seemingly spread out over a quarter of the country, and though his mother-in-law claims they have mountains he thinks she's probably making this up. It's humid and hot, and he meets aunts and uncles and roughly a thousand cousins, only 6 or 7 of whom are apparently not named Bubba, Billy Mac, or Pam. They all come over, to see what she's brung them.

He learns that ponds are "tanks," that potatoes are taters, and that what's really important is God, country, and the Dallas Cowboys, and not always in that order, depending on the time of year.

She takes him on a tour of her life: Her house, her high school, and finally her college, North Texas State in Denton. A state university but with a prestigious, internationally acclaimed college of music. This is for serious students. You come to North Texas as a musician, y'all better have the chops for it.

She did, and does. He smiles when he thinks about the conflicts over the years, the choirs she directs and budgets she projects, and the self-appointed powers-that-be who want to dismiss her as just a pretty voice. She was music student of the year at North Texas, he thinks, at a time when North Texas was the largest school of music in the world. Shut up and learn something.

"Texas?" he says when someone asks. "Yeah, I spent a year there one week," but he's just joking. Texas is fine, there's just no connection for him. Nor is there one with his former states, California and Arizona. He came home 20 years ago, and this is it: The mountains, the Sound, the trees and the rain. This is where he always belonged, he believes, and his children are now natives.

He looks at his favorite picture again. It was taken during a rehearsal for Tacoma Opera's production of "The Magic Flute." She is playing Pamina. She is 31, looking younger than that, with lots of hair, a plaid shirt, blue jeans and the boots. Other cast members are in the background, watching her.

And on her shoulders, in a baby backpack, is her one-year-old daughter, red hair blazing, thumb securely in mouth, apparently unperturbed by the setting or the sound of her mother singing, as if she had been doing it all her life. Which she had.

"Someday," someone could have remarked back then, "that baby will grow up and follow in her mother's footsteps." Her mom would have howled. "Oh, Lord, she'll probably be a chemist." These things happen. Children make their own lives. Prophecies about their futures are bad bets.

Genetics and geography are funny things, though, he thinks as he puts the picture away. And destinies are only clearly seen from the perspective of the future. He will probably think about this often, and especially in August, when he puts his daughter on a plane. North Texas State will get another freshman voice major in the fall, this one a red-haired Northwest native with a will of iron and an impressive pedigree. She will, in a way, be going home.

This is his favorite picture. Just a shutter click in time, it still has power and magic. It holds the middle of one story and the beginning of another. It is a picture of symmetry and cycles. It is a picture of the future hiding in the past, where it always is.

And it's a reminder that his little girl is leaving. He always knew she had to, of course, always knew that she would, and if only he'd paid more attention he would have always known where she was going.

Mars and Venus

I read an article in Time magazine last week that cleared up some things about men and women. Things I suspected, but now know for a fact.

It turns out, from recent studies, that the reason women statistically live years longer than men has less to do with biological differences than intellectual ones. In other words, men die earlier because they do dumb things.

I'm not just talking about bad habits, like smoking and drinking and eating chili-cheese fries by the half-gallon. A man is much more likely, for example, in fact tremendously more likely, to be killed in a flash flood than a woman. Think about that for a minute.

While a woman, at the first hint of a flash flood, which I assume is a pretty good hint, is heading for higher ground, a man is scoffing. "What, afraid of a little WATER? Afraid you'll get your pretty shoes a little WET? Afraid you'll...gasp...gurgle..."

Even in those places where, statistically speaking, flash floods are less likely to occur, such as inside, male dumbness can be seen every day. Your typical man, for instance, will often attempt to move your typical refrigerator all by himself, while his wife stands by and suggests quietly that she get a neighbor to help. "No, I got it," he mutters, as previously non-existent veins start popping out on his forehead and every part of his body that is capable of herniating is doing so.

My wife, like most women, attempts to keep my dumb side from getting me in trouble. This is easier for her than some, maybe, because she loves tools and fooling around with things. Give my wife an unassembled desk and a screwdriver and she is blissfully happy (note to self: wedding anniversary coming up).

I, on the other hand, am not a natural tool user. A few years ago, she gave me one of those stand-alone basketball hoops for Christmas. I took it down to the basement to put together, and after about 12 hours I looked up to find her watching me. "Put down the wrench," she said softly, "and just step away. Real slow and easy. And keep your hands where I can see them."

So I gave up. Now, when I spot the ladder on the back deck and know she's on the roof, cleaning the gutters, I feel no twinges of guilt. I just turn on the TV and let Martha Stewart show me how to make really lovely planters out of recycled plastic. Martha Stewart is amazing.

My manly duties in the household, then, have been reduced to getting things off of high shelves, certain television component-related issues, computer problems, and my daughter's car.

My daughter came out of class last week and found that she had a flat tire, so I was called upon once again. How this happened was interesting. My daughter did not attempt to change the tire herself, or to get one of her many testosterone-laden friends to help, or even to call Dad on her convenient cell phone.

No. That would make too much sense. She got a ride home with a friend, assuming, I guess, that at some point during the night, the Mukilteo Tire Patrol would swing by and fix it. Or else the tire would change its mind and not want to be flat in the morning.

This is how I ended up driving to the high school with my wife one afternoon. My wife was bubbly, maybe just because we were getting out of the house alone together, or maybe because she suspected tools would be involved. I was less bubbly, probably because I noted that it had started to rain.

My wife knew nothing about changing a tire, although that didn't stop her from making suggestions, most of which were pretty good. And whenever I stopped pumping the jack and straightened up to rest my aching back, she'd immediately jump in, loosening lug nuts and humming to herself. This happened several times.

And these few times, me standing up with my hand on my lower back while my wife wrestled with the tire, just happened to coincide with the times that a majority of Harbour Pointe residents chose to drive by the school. Some of them apparently went around the block and came back for a second look.

I comforted my bruised ego, though, with the thought that this is how it's supposed to be, men and women working together, complementing each other's strengths, compensating for each other's weaknesses. And by the second time we changed that tire, we were a real team, working with practically pit crew speed.

We had to change it twice, of course, because it never occurred to me that, before I put it on, it might be a good idea to see if the spare was also flat.

My wife was kind enough not to mention that this was a new level of dumbness for me, but as we headed for the used tire store I couldn't help but think that this never would have happened to Martha Stewart.

School Daze

Let me tell you about my world these days.

Three people I care about have been diagnosed with cancer in the past month or so. There's plenty of hope with all three, but still.

Thanks to my Beacon colleague Larry Simoneaux, I went fishing a couple of weeks ago with my son. First time in years. I caught one, too, although my casting skills need a lot of work.

I'm really concerned about this imminent FCC decision to allow media conglomerates to own large chunks of the system that provides information to most Americans (i.e., newspapers and television). And I'm more concerned from the impression I get that most people don't even know about it.

Bill Bennett has crossed my mind a time or two, as has the Flight Suit In Chief. So has the lady golfer thing, although I don't golf so I didn't pay much attention.

I could write about all of this, and maybe I will. But, for better or worse, I'm a father, and after eighteen and a half years I'm now approaching the end of a chapter. For the next couple of weeks, then, I hope you'll bear with me. I have things on my mind.

If memory serves (and my particular server has been down a lot lately), the last teacher strike in the Mukilteo School District was in the fall of 1990. These are never pleasant, for anyone involved, but as this came before school started it was hardest, I suspect, for the five-year-olds. Eleventh-graders probably enjoyed their additional five weeks of vacation, but those entering kindergarten had been waiting a long time for summer to end.

It was in October, then, that my daughter had her first day of school. My wife drove her, and she noticed that down the block a few houses, another little red-haired girl and her mom were apparently waiting for a bus that hadn't come. My wife stopped and offered them a ride, and this is how my daughter met Lucy.

They were in Mrs. Lien's afternoon kindergarten class at Serene Lake Elementary, and they became friends. The bus situation got straightened out, so every day at noon I'd walk Beth outside and she'd look for Lucy. The two of them would wait together.

Years later, Beth would sometimes drive by and give Lucy a ride to high school. Imagine that.

Time, like most things, is relative. As we all know, relativity was invented by Albert Einstein in 1928. "Sit on a hot stove for a minute," he said, "and it seems like an hour. Spend an hour with a pretty girl, and it seems like a minute. That's relativity."

One suspects Albert Einstein had gotten real tired of answering dumb physics questions.

His statement, though, does bring up some interesting questions. Did he actually test this theory? What if it had been a pretty hot stove?

I get it, though. The past 13 years have been fairly slow for me; lots of routine, some drudgery, some extra pounds, a little less hair, mostly and merely day after day of the same old, same old.

But last week I walked her down to the kindergarten bus. Two days later she went to the Homecoming dance, and the next morning I taught her how to drive. Over the weekend she learned how to play the cello, appreciate good coffee, surf the net, do algebra and speak Russian. Now there are only a few school days left, and I realize my time with a pretty girl seems like only a minute.

Again, I ask for your patience as I blather on about something we all experience. My friend, Paul, who enjoys pointing out my various neuroses, commented once about my obsession with the passing of time. "Time seems to weigh heavier on you," he said (yes, ha ha, very nice, thank you).

There's a lot going on in the world, as always. We haven't found Osama, Saddam, or WMD. SARS is still out there, as is the West Nile virus. I haven't heard about the killer bees lately, but I assume they're still around.

The Mariners are red hot. The economy is still anything but. I haven't seen "The Matrix: Reloaded" but I intend to.

But these days, I'm remembering teachers and T-ball games. School carnivals and choir concerts.

And mostly the image of two red-haired girls. They stand on the street and talk and laugh, and when the bus comes they literally skip their way aboard. I watch it drive away, confident that I know where they're headed, only now understanding that it was not to elementary school, but toward today.

This is my world, then. I spend my days paying for prom dresses and tuition, but in the back of my mind I'm still sort of waiting, halfway listening for a bus that hasn't stopped here in a long time.

The Leader Of The Band

If you're up early enough, you can wander by any high school in the waning days of summer and watch them learn.

This is the stuff of halftime shows and holiday parades, a common sight, but in the beginning things are a little ragged. Even for the veterans, the juniors and seniors, I imagine it takes a while to get the polish back.

I've never done it, so it's probably not as difficult as I think, but trying to march in clean, crisp lines while the dew is still on the grass and your eyes are barely open seems a study in dedication. Not to mention playing an instrument at the same time.

In contrast, I don't even like to have the radio on when I drive. When I take a walk, I leave the chewing gum at home. I'm a unitasker, and I'd never make it in a marching band.

I don't know Anita Valdez, the band director at Explorer, whose students recently won that big first place prize, but it sounds like she's a terrific teacher. I know many parents feel the same way about Mr. Caldwell at Olympic View. There are similar stories, I'm sure, about other music teachers at other area schools.

I write about what I know, though, so I want to talk a bit, here at the end of the school year, about Brian Steves.

I could write about other teachers whose paths have crossed mine through my daughter's adventures in high school. Mr. Costello. Mr. Morris, certainly.

The legendary Ms. Russell, dreaded by graduating eighth-graders and (I suspect) appreciated by college freshmen, who finally understand exactly what she was teaching them. I could write a book about Ms. Russell.

But for many Kamiak seniors, nearly a quarter of their lives have been spent under the influence of Mr. Steves, the band and orchestra director. On behalf of their parents, I just wanted to say thanks.

"Get your children involved in music," a former teacher and friend told me years ago. "They meet a better group of kids."

Well, there are lots of great kids, involved in lots of different activities, but I know what he was talking about. Mastering music requires work and time, lessons hard to learn but valuable as people prepare for real life.

At the Kamiak orchestra concert a few weeks ago, Brian Steves introduced a group of students who had practiced on their own time, selected their own music, corrected and directed each other, and who, in fact, ended up winning third place in the state Solo and Ensemble competition last month, in a highly competitive category.

He talked about their drive and initiative, and the audience responded with sustained applause. Me, too, but I wondered then what I was applauding: these ambitious, dedicated kids, or the man who taught them to be that way?

Both, of course, but we focus on the kids and occasionally forget that there are unsung heroes who deserve sometimes to be serenaded.

He got there early and often stayed late. He counseled and consoled. He taught them how to march and play and play better. I'd guess he probably wasn't paid enough. I'd guess that seldom crossed his mind.

This Thursday, June 12, the Kamiak orchestra will give their final concert. The seniors, following tradition, will be wearing strange clothes. Brian Steves, also following tradition, will try to ignore this.

You might want to come. You'll hear first-rate musicians and music. You'll witness the result of lessons and practice, of study and solitary hours spent in the pursuit of excellence.

There will be a senior moment, and I'll give you a preview, something to watch for. It'll have nothing to do with funny clothes, or flowers or speeches.

It will come toward the end. There will be a moment, then, when breaths are taken and strings go still. Brian Steves will lower his baton for the last time, and the class of 2003 will be done. Watch them closely. Four years will be marked at that moment, in a far more poignant way than just being handed a diploma.

They've become a better group of kids. I know a lot of them. And I've exchanged maybe a dozen words with Brian Steves over the past four years, but I know things, and I write what I know.

If you're the parent of an eighth-grade musician who is planning to attend Kamiak, I know that your child will be in good hands.

And, four years from now, I know you'll be proud of what they've accomplished. They will be better people for their dedication and discipline. They will have learned that hard work is its own reward, but that beautiful music is the bonus.

They will walk across the stage and get their diplomas. Their heads will be held high as they approach the rest of their lives. And if they are marching in clean, crisp lines, it's only because that's what Mr. Steves taught them to do.

Alpha and Omega

"How many more columns are there going to be?" Mary Knoll asked me last week.

I understood. Her son and my daughter have been friends since middle school, and both graduated from Kamiak this past Monday. It was difficult enough for her without having to read my angst in these pages.

"One more," I said, holding up a (polite) finger. "I'm just working some stuff out."

I promise. Next week, I start writing about my lawn again, or my dog, or Hillary or something. Enough is enough.

It's been a hectic week or so. There were parties and farewells, lots of pictures and lots of anxiety. I gather there were some hair and wardrobe issues. No one paid any attention to me at all, which was probably a good thing.

I tried to stay out of the way. I also tried to convince my son to run away from home for a few days, but he just stayed in his room. So I've had time to think.

I was there at the beginning, a literal alpha male. Her first preschool was a converted house on Capitol Hill in Seattle, and sometimes after work I'd walk the few blocks from my office and pick her up.

I seem to recall that it was a glorious spring in 1988, warm and sunny. We'd walk hand in hand through tree-lined streets, talking about her day and about the house we were buying in far-off Snohomish County.

She was all enthusiasm and energy, amazed with the world. "The air is so FRESH," she'd say. "The sky is so BLUE."

I worked a little digital magic last week, combining pictures of Robert Knoll and Beth from freshman year and this year. It was interesting. The physical changes were subtle, but the poise, the inner grace, was there. They've grown up a lot in four years.

And suddenly it struck me. This is what I've been trying to do in the past few weeks, construct a Photoshop montage of her life from preschool to senior prom, and all along I've been focusing on the wrong journey.

Graduation speakers seem compelled to remind us every year that commencement is just another word for beginning. It never feels like that.

I know that parenting doesn't end with high school graduation, but something does, something substantial, and with all the activity recently, it took me a while to realize that all the sentiment and nostalgia was about me.

I used to have this recurring dream about finding a pool in our backyard. Not a wading pool or a plastic pool, but a real-live, honest-to-God built-in pool. It was covered with algae and floating trash and tree branches, and I'd kick myself for forgetting we had it and not taking care of it.

This is what's been really bothering me, then. Because it seems to me that after the first formative years, after we send them off to school and teachers and friends, it matters less what we've taught our children than what they've taught us.

What have I learned? What did I forget to pay attention to? Could I have spent 18 years as a father and learned nothing else than how much car insurance costs and how to go to sleep at night when my daughter is watching TV with a boy in her room?

Oh, I learned how to put dresses on dolls and watch "Sleeping Beauty" 20 times in a row. I learned how to ignore the rolling eyes and the slammed doors. I learned the importance of multiple phone lines.

As I say, I was on my own. My wife and daughter were having a lot of obviously private conversations, or else not speaking to each other. I was not on anyone's agenda.

I walked around the house on Father's Day, eventually ending up on the back deck, and then I found myself thinking about the candy store.

It was just a little mom 'n' pop on the corner, but when she was 3 Beth called it the candy store, for reasons you can probably figure out. It was our place, the Starbuck's of the preschool set, and then I remembered.

They see things that we've begun to miss. They look at life and see pure Creation, alive and waiting for them. Everything is new and radiant, and in watching them grow we learn something we'd forgotten.

I've passed these years working and worrying, sweating the small stuff and having strange dreams, and all the time I was learning from a little girl how to look at the world once again through the eyes of a child. And I thought I was going to teach her. Time to graduate now.

I stand on the back deck, oblivious to the commotion inside, bathed in the glow of a parent's pride and the warmth of another glorious spring. I can see all the corners of my yard. There is no pool, I know, and there never was. There are just beginnings, and endings, and beginnings again.

"The sky is so blue," I say to myself, and of course no one pays any attention to me at all.

Harry and Where the Heart Is

The newest Harry Potter novel, "The Order of the Phoenix," went on sale last Saturday, so I did the prudent thing and headed out of town.

I think Harry Potter books are great, really I do. The idea that millions of kids worldwide are reading instead of watching is encouraging. And not just kids. There are two Potterphiles in my home, and one of them I'm married to.

It's just that watching these two undergo their ritual Potter-a-thon, devouring 900 pages in a single sitting, is sort of like watching my grass grow, except not as much fun.

So I went home, or at least where home used to be.

I lived in Arizona for 14 years, long enough to develop affection for the state and probably triple my risk of skin cancer. Most of that time was spent in Phoenix, the capitol, the Valley of the Sun.

If you think of Arizona as a giant cereal bowl, which is not as easy as it sounds, with Tucson at one rim and Flagstaff at the other, Phoenix is at the bottom. This produces a meteorological effect technically known as "air quality from hell." Bring oxygen.

I went to visit my parents, who live in a mountain community northeast of Phoenix, so I pretty much skirted the city. It's unfamiliar for the most part, anyway; Phoenix has always been a work in progress, with new construction constantly spreading the boundaries and pushing into the desert. This is because after five or six years, most of the buildings start to melt.

It was 95 degrees when I arrived at Sky Harbor Airport, and the shuttle driver claimed they'd been having cool weather. Maybe so. It was 9 o'clock in the morning, though, and even with my Arizona experience I still wondered if God had made a mistake somewhere along the line.

Of course, traveling from this part of the country to Arizona in June is an act of odd judgment, surpassed only by going there in August, which is when I went last time.

Let's be fair, though. The idea that you can fry an egg on the sidewalk is a myth, as an Arizona Republic reporter pointed out last week. The sidewalk absorbs all the heat. You need a frying pan. Then you can do it.

Actually, I suspect you could, on a particularly hot day in the late afternoon, roast a pig on a spit over an Arizona sidewalk.

By the way, according to the U.S. Copyright Office, this Sidewalk Pig Roasting concept now belongs to me. Anyone interested in franchising can contact me in care of this paper.

A visit was overdue, and even though I only had a couple of days we had a good time. We talked and drove around a bit, and in the evenings Mom and I took a walk.

The weather was beautiful at that time of day, cool with a breeze and beautiful blue skies. It took us a while, as my mother apparently knows every dog in the neighborhood and had to stop and chat.

At night we watched movies, prompting Dad once again to wonder aloud what the big deal is about DVD ("When I was a kid, if we wanted to rewind a video we had to crank it by hand!"), but it was a great visit. I treasure my parents, and I'm not grateful enough that they're smart and funny and only mentioned half a dozen times or so that the hair on the back of my head was getting pretty darn thin.

On my return flight, I blew fifty bucks and upgraded to first class, so I sat in a comfy seat and looked out the window at the lights of Phoenix as we took off (it was dark at 8:30 at night, if you can imagine that). Two magazines, two glasses of Chardonnay, and two and a half hours later I looked at the lights of Seattle. They were just as bright, although interrupted by dark patches (for my Arizona readers, all five of you, this was water).

My wife was waiting in the van, having finished with Harry half an hour before, and when I got home my son murmured a sleepy greeting. The dog gave me an accusatory sniff, sensing a breech of a canine commandment ("You've been with another dog!").

I brushed my teeth with my regular toothbrush, checked my email on my own computer, and slept in my own bed, glad to be back and glad to have gone. I don't go there nearly enough, and it reminded me of all the good things about the place I grew up: the smell of orange blossoms in the spring and early summer, the clear skies, the friends and family I love.

And it also reminded me of the lesson I learn every time I travel. I watched out the window as we made our approach to the airport, slipping north past SeaTac and banking over downtown Seattle, and on this summer solstice I saw blue sky to the west at just after 11 p.m.

With apologies to Thomas Wolfe, you can always go home again. You just need to remember where home really is, and who is waiting for you there.

Mary and Madelynne

We're allowed to wander during weddings. There's a bit of a liturgical license to think about other things, because we know what's going to happen. There will be rings, and a kiss, and possibly an open bar at the reception.

This is part of the joy in our traditions and rituals, the comfort of familiar words and symbols. We can float in and out, absorbing the sight and at the same time marveling at how blue the Sound looks in the background.

I had several things on my mind, then, this past Saturday, when I watched Mary get married.

Mary Eidbo is my one of daughter's oldest friends, and she's been a presence in my home for years. Since we don't actually allow most people to come inside, you know she's special.

So I was thinking of different things. Watching Marty Eidbo walk her down the aisle and fight emotions as he gave an eloquent fatherly speech, I thought a lot about the merits of daughters just eloping.

Rev. Mark Smith performed the ceremony, and I found myself remembering when he baptized my children, so many years ago.

I thought about the beauty of the day and of my wife and daughter, as they sang together. The bride looked stunning and so did the sky. I wondered about sunscreen.

And, on this day of beginnings, I thought about Madelynne.

Madelynne Martin was born the morning of Mary's wedding, across the country in the other Washington. She is my second cousin, 45 years my junior and firstborn to Jay and Angela.

Jay is the son of my mother's sister, making him my cousin technically and my little brother in all other senses. Ten years younger than I, born three weeks after the assassination of Robert Kennedy in the summer of 1968, Jay has always been one of my favorite people.

So I rejoiced a bit at the news that he was a father this Saturday, and as I watched young people get married I also thought about a little girl, born in her nation's capitol at the beginning of a new century. And I imagined.

She will know nothing of an analog world. Camera film and rotary dial phones will be relics, museum pieces. Her entire life will be videotaped.

She will be the class of 2021, and the Twenties will be her 20s.

The first U.S. President she is really aware of will be elected in 2016. Somewhere along the line, at least one of them will be a woman, jettisoning that particular bugaboo once and for all.

When she is in her 30s, Bill Clinton will be buried, probably yapping to the end, charming and infuriating, the last president of the 20th century.

At 42, she will mark with others the hundredth anniversary of the end of the Second World War and the last time a nuclear weapon was used in anger. She will be grateful.

When she's 50, Keanu Reeves will get a Lifetime Achievement award at the Oscar ceremony, mostly because he outlived Matt Damon. "Bill and Ted's Excellent Adventure" will be incomprehensible to her.

George Carlin will not ring a bell, or Bob Hope. Jerry Seinfeld will mean nothing to her, and Jay Leno will be an encyclopedia entry.

Jack Benny and Sid Caesar will be remembered as giants.

The New York Yankees will move to Minnesota and fade away, the Seattle Mariners will win 20 straight World Series, and in 2048 Edgar Martinez will be the first octogenarian to hit 30 doubles and 100 RBIs in a single season.

I'm just making stuff up now.

Maybe her parents will write down what was happening in the world when she was born. Iraq. Globalization. New diseases. Strange weather.

Maybe they'll mention that she entered this world as Katharine Hepburn left it, 96 years young.

And if she takes care of herself, eats her vegetables and crosses with the light, when she's 96 Madelynne will see a new century turn.

Our world will be dust then, but it welcomes you today, Madelynne Martin, 7 pounds, 3 ounces. We've given you most of a century to play with, so you go, girl.

I'm just a remote relative, stuck up here in my little corner of the country. I think it's unlikely I will play any part in your life, or even that you will quite understand who I am.

But, when you're a grown woman and I'm an old man, and you're a little curious about the day you were born, feel free to look me up. I will remember.

It was a beautiful day up here, sunny and warm, and Puget Sound was bright and blue. I stood in the sun and toasted not only a marriage but also a birth, long ago when the century and you were new.

Freedom's Just Another Word For...

To many of us, the nicest words in the English language are, "Have you lost weight?"

Actually, it can be toss-up between those and, "Do you want the rest of my sandwich?" but I give the edge to the former.

I heard it maybe half a dozen times last Sunday, and I'm still writing thank-you notes, but it reminded me I was supposed to check in with you about now. It's been four months or so since I announced in this space my intention to do a little personal downsizing. Call it 18 weeks. Or, better yet, call it around 60 pounds. That sounds so much better.

I thought about piling 60 pounds of books, say, in a cardboard box and carrying that around the house for a while to help remind me of what I've lost, but it sounded like too much work. Besides, I'm pretty busy trying on pants. I do that a lot.

We're obsessed in America with our bodies, partly because we baby boomers are aging and we're generally obsessed with ourselves anyway, but mostly because we've become a nation of porkers.

For a long time, we were told this was because we ate too much fat. Fat makes you fat, they chided us, Richard Simmons and the rest, and we paid attention. We switched from ice cream to frozen yogurt. We threw out the mayo and stuck with mustard. America cut back on the fat. And we got bigger.

So we started buying stuff, mostly off TV. Rowers and walkers and riders, ab toners and treadmills. You've got at least one of these around the house, if not three. Sure you do. It's under all that laundry that needs to be folded.

Therefore, being the outstanding public servant that I am, I did a little investigating, turning myself into a human guinea pig for the sake of society, and I learned the secret to taking weight off and keeping it off. And I'll pass it on, as soon as I remember what it is.

Oh, yeah. Don't eat so much.

There you go. You don't have to thank me.

Fat didn't make us fat, you see. Calories did. Lots of them, more than we need, sometimes more than several people need. America wants more, or at least that's what the restaurateurs and food marketers think, so they supersized and so did we.

Take one of those big bottles of any popular soft drink. You know, the one-liter variety that's all over the convenience stores. My son can polish one of these off at a single setting. I could, too. Now let's look at the vital statistics: Over 100 grams of carbohydrate (all sugar; no fiber here), 120 milligrams of sodium, and (wait for it) 400 calories. But hey, it's fat free.

Add to larger portions an acquired American taste for white, fluffy bread, deep frying and lots of sugar, and compare that to an average diet of, say, 100 years ago, and at the end of my vast research I came to a startling conclusion: It wasn't the Big Mac that made us fat. It was the Coke and fries, and I'm not letting the bun off the hook, either.

Those of you wise in the ways of contemporary weight loss philosophy might right about now be suspecting a little anti-carbohydrate bias. It's true that I started off trying the controlled-carb Atkins approach, and it worked fine. Actually, it was great.

The choices can be limiting, though, unless you really work at it, and so I ended up eating a lot of the same foods, thus proving my Twinkie Diet Theory (you can lose weight eating only Twinkies, widely considered the most fantastic non-naturally occurring food in the universe, as eventually you will stop eating altogether because you're busy writing threatening Unabomber-style letters to the Hostess corporation. You'll hate the sight of Twinkies, which doesn't seem possible but you just have to trust me).

So, after a few weeks of 20 gm of carbs a day, mostly from vegetables, and a growing lack of interest in eating anything, I added back in fruit (berries) and nuts, and then after 40 pounds or so I got preoccupied and stopped working on it.

And I kept losing. Because I didn't eat as much as I used to. Funny.

I didn't reach an impasse, I didn't start gaining again, I just eased into a steady one or two pounds a week of weight loss without really thinking about it. I had finally learned, after all these years, what my grandmother (or Ben Franklin, or Thoreau) could have told me: Moderation in most things is usually a good idea, and pays the most benefits.

So, class, let's sum up. You want to drop some extra pounds?

Don't eat so much. Move more. Stay away from sugar. Learn to like leafy green vegetables, or at least tolerate them. Try on pants a lot. Read this column every week.

And feel free to ask me if I've lost weight. Go ahead, I'll tell you all about it. My pleasure. Although I guess I've already done that. So maybe I should just shut up. Yes, I think so. Definitely. Shutting up now.

Chasing Chevy

We tend to think of humor as universal and constant; we've always laughed at the same sort of things, we think, from Shakespeare to Saturday Night Live, but this isn't entirely true.

Humor is also evolutionary, topical and even transitional, changing with cultures and the way we think about our lives. Some things aren't funny anymore, and we wonder how they ever were.

Same thing with comedians. We get used to them, get used to their timing and shtick, and we want something new. We can be fickle.

So it was a pleasure to see Sid Caesar on "Larry King" a few weeks ago. I laughed a lot, and I'm a hard laugh to get.

At 80, he looked decades younger and was as funny as ever. I'm actually not sure what was better, watching him improvise with Larry or seeing the clips from "Your Show of Shows," fifty years earlier and recently restored.

It was before my time, but I've seen some of it and always found it funny, even after all these years. And why not? Talent surrounded Caesar, writing and performing: Carl Reiner, Howard Morris, Neil Simon, and Mel Brooks, even Woody Allen for a time. When they call 1950s television The Golden Years, "Show of Shows" was a large reason why.

Then there was Imogene Coca. She passed away a year or so ago, and her career never quite matched her Caesar days, but Imogene Coca laid the groundwork for Carol Burnett and the ones who came later. Lucy was a bigger name, but Coca had more range. She was the perfect partner, just as quick and just as funny as Sid.

As I say, Sid Caesar and his company were of a different generation. I came of age with Robin Williams, John Belushi, Steve Martin, Andy Kaufman, and to some extent George Carlin (he was an evolver, and bridged two eras). This was the age of conceptual humor, an outgrowth of the 60s, taunting convention and a lot of times really funny. Some of them will have legacies, and some won't.

Thinking about this reminded me of something that happened 20 years or so ago, though, and about comedy and celebrity and mostly about how I stupid I can be.

My wife and I were working at a dinner theater in Northern Arizona over the summer. It was just tourist entertainment, songs and skits, but I made (I think) 50 bucks a night plus tips, and I wasn't flipping burgers. I had a lot of fun.

One night, Chevy Chase came in for dinner. He'd been making a movie in the area, and he slipped in for a steak at the end of what I assume was a long day.

He didn't come to see our show, but just sat in the dining room next door. I snuck around during breaks to try to get a glimpse, and I just hoped he had a leisurely dinner and would still be there after our final bows.

Our audiences were mostly visitors from the RV park next door, but they always seemed to enjoy the show. As we finished our final number that night, and I was eying the exit, hoping that Chevy was still eating, in the middle of the audience an elderly woman was standing up and hollering "Bravo!" People did this sometimes, and as cast members it was part of our job to mingle, thank them, etc.

So this was my chance, and I took it. Everyone headed for this nice old lady, and I snuck through the door, raced through the bathrooms, and still in costume I caught up with Chevy as he was heading out the door.

He was taller than I thought, wearing a baseball cap. He pretended to walk into a wall for the benefit of the few of us hanging around, and then he was out the door. My brush with greatness.

You could call Chevy Chase the Sid Caesar of his generation, I suppose, but you'd probably have to owe him money or be related to him. I don't mean to be hypercritical, but his career, aside from a few hot spots, has been spotty and pretty mediocre. I wanted to see a famous comedian, though, and you never know when you'll get a chance.

You never know.

Looking back now, I just shake my head. I've learned, I hope, to have a better appreciation of talent, and longevity and endurance. I've learned that the flash of the moment is sometimes just that, a flash, and that time will tell.

Seeing Sid Caesar the other night reminded me of that. It reminded me that people who make us laugh should be treasured, particularly when they've done it for a long time and are really good at it.

And it reminded me of the night 20 years ago, the night I chased after Chevy, too young and too dumb to imagine that a little old lady in the other room might have had an idea or two about comedy.

The night Imogene Coca gave us a standing ovation, and I missed it.

Schnebley Hill Road

If my honesty is going to be questioned, my ethics suspected, my credentials challenged, I really would like it to be by someone I don't like. And preferably by someone who's wrong, too.

When it's a family member, and more than one, it hurts. I've got feelings like anybody else.

This happens from time to time. People have accused me of all sorts of things after I've written columns, and, as Dorothy said about elements of Oz, some of them aren't very nice.

But I wrote a column two weeks ago about a chance encounter with Chevy Chase and a missed meeting with Imogene Coca, and both my mother and my brother had a question, which essentially was, "Did you make that up?"

My own mother.

I can see where there's room for doubt. Two famous people show up in a little dinner theater in Flagstaff, Arizona in the early 1980s on the same night? What are the odds?

Of course, if one (no one in particular, now) were to simply go to the Internet Movie Database and enter "Chevy Chase," then pair him with Imogene Coca, the answer would pop up immediately.

"National Lampoon's Vacation," released in 1983. Click on "filming locations" and you find three sites in Northern Arizona, one of them the Grand Canyon and another Flagstaff.

But these are only statistics. There's got to be a little trust, people.

Like anyone who's reached my stage of life and finds that the names of his kids sometimes go missing and his keys are always somewhere else, my memory can be faulty. And from time to time I exaggerate a situation for a joke, or compress events to save room, but I do not make stuff up. OK, mom?

I actually went to IMDB to check this little experiment out, and I realized that the third filming location in Arizona for that movie was a story, too, and that my chasing Chevy episode had a little coda.

Schnebley Hill Road runs east-west, from downtown Sedona, Arizona to I-17. It has great vistas of red rock formations, but it's unpaved and bumpy and has little car traffic. I'd guess it'd be ideal for filming, capturing a little Southwest color without a crowd.

In the Schnebley scene, the Clark Griswald family is traveling west toward Walley World when they discover that Grandma (Coca) in the backseat has ceased to exist, so to speak. Kicked the bucket. Shuffled off this mortal coil.

Brakes are slammed and the four viable Griswalds exit in a timely fashion. Push "pause" now. This is the exact spot, an insignificant mark in the middle of nowhere, on Schnebley Hill Road, where 20 years ago today I got married.

Honestly. I have pictures and everything.

By "today" I mean Wednesday, the day this paper is published. You may be reading this after the fact. You could still send a card or something. No problem.

We didn't realize our wedding spot would be a part of cinematic history. We just thought it was pretty, and we had to get married somewhere.

We didn't HAVE to get married. You know what I mean.

It was small, some friends and family. My father-in-law hung wind chimes on a tree branch and the breeze provided our music. It was a short wedding, perhaps because that part of the country is famous for midday summer storms and the clouds looked threatening; maybe the minister rushed it a little.

My brother and his family, driving up from Phoenix, actually missed the vows, so maybe this is why he questioned my Chevy story, I don't know. Maybe he has doubts about whether I'm actually married.

I am.

I know a 25th anniversary is "silver," and that a 50th is "gold." I was told what the 20th is but I forgot. It would be nice if it was "cash" but that's probably not the case.

I have no explanations for how we made it 20 years, other than by turning calendar pages and hanging on for dear life. Our road has occasionally been unpaved and bumpy, too, but there have also been some spectacular vistas. Births. Friends. Challenges. Laughter and music.

So we can sigh a little today, take a deep breath, and look at where we've been, and whom.

I have no insight into the future, but I remember the past all right. If 20 years have dimmed some details, I still know the important things. It was a Saturday, July 30, 1983. It was a day that started off sunny and then gradually grayed. It was a working day, with a show to do that night. It was a day we shared with my grandmother, marking her birthday.

It was the day we got married on the side of Schnebley Hill Road, simply and quietly, late in the morning, surrounded by people who loved us, exchanging inexpensive rings and serious words, finishing just minutes before it began to rain.

The Boys of Summer

I turn 45 this week, and I've learned something recently. At 45, you can't really fool yourself into pretending you're still somewhere around 30, because you're not. At 45, it turns out you're exactly midway between 40 and another place that I'm not going to talk about.

I learned this because last weekend, my friend Dave and I spent the first 10 minutes of our annual road trip talking about our teeth.

Even a year ago, I couldn't have imagined spending even five minutes on dental issues, but we were just getting warmed up when we mutually agreed to stop because it was freaking us out. Talk about lower back pain and bladder problems seemed just around the corner, and we wanted to play loud music and laugh and party like we were young, and maybe take a nap in the afternoon.

Although we did have a brief conversation about vasectomies. That's OK, because after a few minutes of that you really want to talk about something else, anyway.

Dave is three months younger and about an inch taller, just as he was when we met 30 years ago in the hallway at our high school and I made fun of his hat.

It actually was probably a very "cool" hat, or "hip" or maybe "the cat's pajamas" (I can't remember how we talked in high school, so I get confused. We said "far out" a lot as I recall). It was black with a wide brim, though, so I took to calling him "Zorro" and he didn't seem to mind as long as he sensed, you know, some respect for the hat.

Sarcasm seems a strange way to start a relationship, but 30 is a long time in friend years so there must have been something. If you were to graph our separate tastes and interests, the lines would intersect only briefly. He'd no more go to church or a baseball game than I'd spend 8 hours watching European spy films, but we share a common history. We remember old girlfriends, apartments and jobs, weddings and promotions and one particular night that we rarely talk about because neither of us can really remember it, but I think we were 19 and it involved a case of beer.

We didn't pass through Portland this year but stayed there, meeting Bill and all three of us getting rooms with balconies on the banks of the Columbia River. We've done this for years, getting away for a summer weekend with old friends, but this one was the best, for various, circumstantial reasons. Things just went our way.

We had our usual close encounters with waitresses. Every year, there are waitresses who flirt, joke, or insult us, and sometimes all three. We got a trifecta this year, and it just felt right.

We are a motley band of brothers but we're a band, and we walked through the market and downtown, to the waterfront and back, finding a good parking spot and a great Irish pub, accidentally running into a parade with bagpipes and discovering a place to stay next year, when we'll do it all over again.

My brother says he looks forward to these trips to remember how to laugh, and that's a good enough reason for me. I laughed all weekend, mostly at how fortunate we were to be there, to be having fun, and to find what we were looking for, even if we were a little unsure of what it was until we found it. We should have bought lottery tickets; it was our weekend.

I've written about these trips with the boys before, and more than one guy I know has expressed, sort of wistfully, that he'd like to come along, even knowing the dynamics wouldn't be the same. I guess it does seem a little strange, middle-aged men heading out of town with no real destination, no salmon fishing or off-road racing or kayaking to do.

We just pass the time with familiar faces, as time passes us, and we comment on that and other facts of life, but mostly we just remember how to laugh.

Dave got a new hat on this trip, as did Bill. I got new shorts and some socks. We all got sunburns. We went to bed before midnight and brushed after every meal.

One minute after we headed for home we were back in Washington, which made me laugh again. We wanted to go some place else, but as soon as we got there we stopped. That was far enough. The whole trip, in fact, was far out, which was something we used to say a long time ago, when we were really boys, when friendships were forged, and when the last thing on our minds was teeth.

Preachers I Know

Thunder and lightning at 2 o'clock in the morning reminded me that this August was going to be different. As if I needed reminding.

August is supposed to be our summer, when everyone goes on vacation, when we light the barbecue and buy school clothes. For many of us, our internal calendars are set on Labor Day as the true beginning of the year, so in August the kids get antsy and the parents count the days and it's warm and sunny and we do not have thunderstorms, period.

And it's not supposed to be about goodbyes.

It always has been, of course; I'm just new at this. In the next couple of weeks, several families I know are getting ready for the big goodbye. My daughter and many of her friends are fanning out across the country to college, to the Deep South or the Bay Area, Rhode Island or Texas, Montana or Missouri.

And this week, I say goodbye to my friend Roger Rice.

Roger's been a Mukilteo resident for four years or so, but now he's packing his bags and heading east, joining his wife, Judy, in New York, where she now works and lives.

Judy's my friend, too, although mostly we interact online. I send her late night emails about my goofy life and she sends me New York Times articles to read.

Roger Rice, by the way, is the pastor of First Presbyterian Church in Everett. I know a lot of ministers, actually. Thinking about it here, I can come up with nine or ten, and I'm probably forgetting a couple.

I got a new one a few months ago, another friend with a divinity degree and a every-Sunday job. This one is different, to the extent that I don't know his name or where he lives, exactly. He's a virtual preacher to me, but a real live one just the same.

As with so many things on the Internet, I ended up finding Real Live Preacher by accident. Or the grace of God, whatever.

Real Live Preacher is a blogger, and a well-known one (a blogger writes a blog, which is short for web log; you may know this but some people don't. A blog can be about anything or everything). After only nine months of online writing, RLP now gets 800-1200 hits a day. That's a lot of readers.

He's a West Texas minister in his early 40s, married with three daughters. We've exchanged emails for a while now, mostly about writing but some about theological issues.

I suspect there's symbiosis at his site, which is why it works. On one hand, we get a glimpse into the life of someone who has chosen to serve God and us in a hands-on way, and we are ministered to in a church where we can sit wherever we like. Every few days he delivers issues and exegeses and welcomes all, including agnostics, atheists, pagans and people just looking for something to do.

On the other hand, I think his anonymity provides a safe place for him, a site where he can express his frustrations, doubts, and worries, and occasionally slip in a mild profanity to remind us that he's just a guy, too, working his way through. People love the Preacher.

And, oh yeah. He writes like the wind.

We seem to be more suspicious of religious people these days, particularly leaders. Priests who prey on children and TV evangelists who plead for money have made us cynical. This is why, I believe, Real Live Preacher is a hit; he reminds us that in the guts of any inner city church, synagogue, mosque or meeting place are men and women who are other-directed.

You might be surprised to find not a caricature, but a real person. No Reverend Lovejoy or Jerry Falwell here. You will find a person who turns on the heat in the morning and locks the doors at night. Someone who passes the days in hospital corridors and nursing homes, who worries about utility bills and parking problems. People like you and me, but different. People like Real Live Preacher and Roger Rice.

I have great affection for them, these people who commit their lives to servicing the rest of us, showing us light in the darkness and telling us we are loved. I don't think you have to be a believer to appreciate that for every sleazy salesman hawking scripture on TV, for every jihad-calling theocrat, for every gay-bashing buffoon who claims a direct line to God, there are thousands of others who just worry that people don't have enough food, or money, or support.

You can find the Preacher at reallivepreacher.com. You can find Roger Rice at First Presbyterian on Rockefeller and Wall Street this Sunday, as he says goodbye. You can find me there, too, sad that he's leaving, glad to have known him, and grateful that there are people like him in this world, and that I know some of them, virtually or otherwise.

Bethy Was Here

Well, the girl is gone.

Packages were shipped and suitcases were stuffed, and Beth and her mom headed to Texas last week.

This left a household of male inhabitants, begging the question: How many consecutive nights can you eat pizza for dinner? We are heading into uncharted territory.

I'm including Strider, who also eats pizza, although he steals it. He apparently has no ethical qualms about this.

Strider is the dog that lives in my house. While I take some responsibility for the planning and conception of my children (my wife insists I was there), Strider is not my dog. Strider was researched, sought, bred and bought over my objections.

I said we were too unorganized to take care of a dog. I tried to explain this once to a lady I knew. "We can't even keep the bathroom clean," I said.

She gave me a pitying look. "You know, the dog won't use the bathroom," she said, and I knew I'd lost.

I feel sorry sometimes for Strider. He's a Sheltie, a Shetland sheepdog, and hundreds of years of breeding have left him looking for something to herd. There are no sheep in my house, and my kids were already fairly independent by the time he arrived.

His job in life was over before it started, then, so he's an unemployed dog. For all I know, when he's alone in the house he watches soap operas and drinks wine that comes in a box.

Sometimes, he'll sit outside my office door and cry. I know it's probably just a howl, but it sounds like crying to me. It's a mournful sound, high and sustained. I used to open the door and try to comfort him, but now I just tell him to shut up. My sympathy has limits.

Strider wasn't around 15 years ago when we bought this house. In a picture I took back then, Beth is running like crazy down the driveway with a wild grin on her face.

Over the years, she gave that driveway a workout. A tricycle, a wagon, a bike, then that 1986 Lynx we bought for $1000 when she got her driver's license. It was a good starter car with low mileage and a nice stereo, and she destroyed it. Just drove it into the ground. Now it sits in my garage, leaking transmission fluid and oil and something that sort of looks like blood. But it got her where she was going.

So it's a change. Our household will be different. We sent Texas a smart, funny, personable and talented young woman, and at Christmas I assume we'll get her back, probably sunburned and talking funny.

"I know I'll be fine," Beth said on more than one occasion about leaving for college. "It's YOU I'm worried about."

This is different, though, less sentiment and more excitement. True, I dropped her at the airport early in the morning, came home and went into her nearly empty bedroom. I sat there for a few minutes, remembering. Then I moved her TV into my room.

I've realized something, though. It turns out that all these years, during my dumb choices and bad behavior and regrets and mistakes, running through my mind, just beneath the surface, was a constant imperative: Get the girl grown.

Let her do well in school, let her have good friends and enjoy her teenage years, let her be spared trauma, let there be enough money, and please God let her get grown before I mess something up and everyone figures out that I haven't got a clue about how to be a parent.

See, your wife takes a test one day and the world changes. You make her toast when she has morning sickness and drive her to the hospital late one night, you learn how to change diapers and heat formula, you sit on tiny plastic chairs for parent-teacher conferences and watch a lot of soccer games, you try to help with homework and attend orchestra concerts, and then she goes to Texas and the world changes again.

I should be relieved, and I guess I am. And I have a son, of course, and bills to pay and a wife to apologize to and this dumb dog. I have jobs; it's just that one of them is done, and I've noticed an empty feeling that wasn't there before.

The house seems awfully quiet. That's just my imagination, though; if I concentrate I can hear things.

My son's tapping his foot upstairs, working his way through the mechanics of a computer game. My neighbors are murmuring in their backyard, trucks rumble down the street, and the fan whirrs over my left shoulder. And I hear the sound of Strider.

He's a good dog, really he is, intelligent and loyal. Right now, as I type these words, he's crying outside my office door, and all of a sudden I think I know why.

In Lieu Of Flowers

It is a dark and stormy night. A night when the numerals on the bedside clock slide by common sense and become absurd. You go to bed at 10 and your clock tells you it's 1:23 and it's only been 5 minutes. The creaking of the house starts to sound like a telltale heart beating, and you realize that if you're a private detective and someone murders your partner, you have to do something even if you don't like him, although you stick your neck out for nobody. But wherever there's a cop beating up a guy you'll be there, and there's a signpost up ahead. Somewhere in the distance, a dog is barking.

A really obnoxious dog.

What runs through your mind when you can't sleep is deadly trivia, the stuff that comes out only in the dark and quiet. You start thinking about old movie dialogue and baseball stats, you try to remember the name of that guy who sat next you in English class, you attempt to list the entire bridge crew of the original "Star Trek" and you forget Chekov, and pretty soon you've got a lot on your mind. You either do something else or plan on watching the sunrise.

So it occurred to me that there might be a window open in the basement, and that now might be a good time to close it.

Our basement used to be a family room, then a master bedroom, and now it's an attic. It's filled with broken furniture and old lamps and a VCR that might or might not work, I can't remember. The floor is strewn with the remnants of almost 20 years of kids: Disney videos, picture books, stuffed animals.

Suddenly I was thinking about my brother.

A few years ago, my brother moved from Phoenix to a small town in Oregon, from Metropolis to Mayberry. This was a town you could do on foot, no sweat. A ten-minute walk from City Hall to what passes for suburbs, and that includes stopping at the store for a cold can of Foster's.

He explored, then, walking in the mornings or after work or on weekends. So sooner or later he was bound to find the cemetery.

A small town cemetery is a good place to stretch your legs, walk under the shade and stir up stories that don't belong to you. He browsed in this beautiful place, lush and green, enjoying the serenity of his surroundings, and then he saw the toys.

Listen: A father of four sees toys carefully placed in front of a tombstone and he really doesn't want to go any further. What he really wants is to turn around and head back the way he came.

They were familiar figures. Luke Skywalker. Batman. A ninja turtle, some Legos, a truck. That's a story you don't want to imagine; you don't want to let your mind wander and fill in the gaps. You don't want to think about parents, about grandma and grandpa and siblings.

A few months later, I sat on his front porch and he told me the story. If it hadn't been my brother, if I hadn't known him to be a thoughtful and honest man, I might have thought "folklore" and forgotten it. As it is, I can't forget. I've told the story before. I will do it again.

It was eerie, to me, at first. My mind wandered to black-and-white movies, to "Psycho" and "Whatever Happened To Baby Jane?" I thought about Norma Desmond ready for her close-up, existing in the present but only alive in the past. And I kept thinking about Who. A mother? A brother? Whoever it was, their grief was overwhelming and a little scary, maybe even neurotic. It took me a while to realize I was wrong.

Even children, with a little coaching, will tell you that a cemetery is not about death. It's about remembering. And once I thought about that a bit, once I realized it wasn't a story about grief, then I understood Who.

Someone who loved a child.

This is not Hallmark card love. This is not even love inscribed on a tombstone. This is force-of-nature love, palpable love, love that grabs the world by the collar and forces us to listen. Listen, this love says: Once, there was a little boy. Remember.

I am in awe of this love.

My brother has returned several times. There have been changes; Spiderman will show up, or a collection of match cars. Someone has been tending the grave.

I know nothing about this story, except what it is. A child was buried and someone remembers, and he will now be forever young. As he was when he died, in a small town in southern Oregon, which, according to the tombstone, was in 1945.

Funny what you think about when you can't sleep.

The Boy On Elm Street

Maybe he thought it would be a parade. Maybe that's what his dad told him. "It's sort of a parade, Joe," something like that. A five-year-old could grasp that. Maybe he thought there would be elephants.

He was my age then and now, if he's alive. What memories he might have of that day I can only speculate on, but I suspect they're fleeting and confused, now meshed with grainy footage and his father's story. As for me, I remember glimpses only, and mostly that there were no cartoons Saturday morning. Five isn't really that old.

His father had already been an eyewitness to history, an Army Ranger on the beach and behind the hedgerows on D-Day. He would be an honoree in France in 1985 and 1995. He would also return to Dealey Plaza from time to time, with less fanfare.

Charles Brehm is a familiar name to JFK assassination buffs, a solid story that never changed until his death in 1996. Wounded in World War II, the victim of a bullet that passed through his body and struck his arm, he would actually be among the first to suggest the "magic bullet" theory, that the first shot hit both Kennedy and John Connelly, although he kept his speculation mostly to himself.

You can find him in the footage, a middle-aged man who describes what he saw on that day in Dallas, listen as he hopes aloud that the President survived but suspects the worst. He was no stranger to violence or gunfire, and perhaps that's why it's the father's fear that resonates over the years. "I pushed my boy down," he says, and his voice quavers.

It's easy to forget that there were children there. The packrat mentality of contemporary American history keeps our scrapbooks bulging with images of that day in 1963. A triple overpass. A grassy knoll. An unremarkable warehouse with a window on the sixth floor. Blurred Secret Service agents. A woman in a pink suit, scrambling for a piece of her husband's skull.

And the culture of conspiracy theory has made the witnesses into icons. Babushka Lady. Umbrella Man. The Tramps. The Epileptic. The Man in the Yellow Jacket. There should be a board game (there probably is).

But there was also a little boy, whose father shoved him to the grass. I wonder about him sometimes.

If Joe Brehm had a story to share, we'd have heard it by now. More likely, his memories are of the days and years that followed, as his father became a magnet for historians and wackos and reporters and the just plain curious. Some were not very nice.

"Your father is a goddamn liar!" they'd scream over the phone at one of Charles Brehm's kids unfortunate enough to answer. For Brehm insisted until his death that there were three shots, that one of them missed high and wide, and that all three came from above him and to the left. In other words, from the School Book Depository.

This is probably part of Joe's story, then. Growing up as a silent witness, maybe remembering little of that day, seeing the aftermath in his own home, maybe wondering what actually happened.

And what did? Forty years later and most Americans still wonder. Six seconds on a sunny autumn day produced an assassination industry that still thrives, as anyone who's watched television this week knows. Serious questions remain, perhaps blocked forever by Jack Ruby's outstretched arm and a street sign in front of Abraham Zapruder's camera.

And what of the legacy of JFK? Would Vietnam still have scarred a generation had he lived? Would Richard Nixon have resurrected himself at the end of a second Kennedy term? Would we have been spared the cynicism engendered by the Warren Commission and Watergate?

I don't dwell on these questions anymore, but once I did. Once I thought about them a lot. Because I was a witness, too.

Like Kennedy, I'm a generational chauvinist. I believe my contemporaries and I have a unique perspective on our national trauma, and that it changed us.

We were too young to understand the details, to even really comprehend what a President was, but old enough to understand death and bullets. We watched from the corners, out of the sight and minds of occupied parents, sneaking peeks at the television from the hallway. Something bad had happened, we knew that. There were no cartoons.

This is why I take note every November 22. This is why I went to Dealey Plaza 20 years ago, just to look around. This is why I stop when there's a clip of a Kennedy press conference or speech on TV, and watch for a moment. This is why I wonder about Joe. Because I remember, too.

Charles Brehm knew they were gunshots. He saw the blood and brains. He pushed his son to the grass on Elm Street and shielded him with his own body, as a father would, thinking he was protecting him, not understanding that it was probably too late.

Witness

I know your secret.

I don't know you personally. I don't know your age, or your gender, your station in life or the color of your eyes. But I know something about you, something I suspect you'd rather I didn't know. I've insinuated myself into your life, then, in a slight way. I've become part of your story, whether you're aware of it or not. I know what you did.

It didn't have to be me, but it probably would have been someone. Maybe not; it all happened so fast, and it was getting late and the roads weren't crowded. I was there, though.

I saw you change lanes in front of me, quickly and without a signal. In fact, I had the impression you were making a last-minute right turn, except there was no place to turn. I watched you repeat this a couple of times, head sideways toward the curb and then correct.

I've seen driving like this before, although fortunately not very often. It always takes me by surprise; the lack of control seems an aberration, almost a breach of the laws of nature. You're supposed to drive straight; that's why there are lines on the road.

I've seen cars weave and over-correct, then do it again and again. I usually watch with disbelief; it takes a few moments, apparently, for my brain to put two and two together, as if I doubt my eyes. Maybe it's a reluctance to pass judgment, although that's never stopped me before.

At any rate, I haven't seen this a whole lot, and until the other night the few times I had the problem disappeared before I decided what to do, if anything, about it. The car turns, or takes the off-ramp, or disappears.

But you, my friend, you were special. You had some serious guidance issues. Your car and you were not on the same page. It wanted to go one way and you weren't exactly putting up a fight. So I got a little show.

I stayed out of your lane and inched closer to you. I had finally clicked into good citizen mode and tried to read your license plate. It was dark and rainy, but I managed to get the first couple of numbers when you did a remarkable thing.

You did that little familiar sideways slide to the curb again, then rolled up on the sidewalk and hit a guy.

Gravity, as a force of nature, is pretty puny if you think about it. A child can defy it, holding a rubber ball in a small hand. A simple kite will sneer at gravity, or a Frisbee.

This young man and you had a little experiment in gravity, then. You hit him. He left the ground. Just went flying through the air. It was an amazing sight, but you didn't seem all that interested. You just headed down the road in the rain. I never even saw brake lights.

Some people found his shoes about 75 yards south of where he landed, by the way. As I say, gravity isn't all it's cracked up to be.

I pulled over. I ran back to the crumpled body, punching 911 on my cell phone and finding myself slipping into TV cop-speak ("A pedestrian is down! I repeat..."). I was the only one who saw. I stood in the rain, waiting for the ambulance and then the police, shivering. And it wasn't that cold.

So, we have something in common now, you and I. We shared a moment in time, two strangers who passed in the night. I know what you did.

Your secret's safe with me. I gave a description, of course, but it wasn't a lot of help. A white compact, maybe a Toyota. A couple of license numbers. You got away with it; I would have heard otherwise, I'm sure.

There are reasons you could have been impaired. Medical reasons, even. Or maybe you pulled a double shift and could barely keep your eyes open; it happens. The fact that you nonchalantly drove off, though, makes me pretty sure you were drunk.

You might be surprised to learn I have some compassion for you. Good and decent people make mistakes, particularly when it comes to alcohol. In a perfect world, people who've had too much to drink would never get behind the wheel of a car, but I see no signs as yet of a perfect world. So bad things sometimes happen, even to good and decent people who make mistakes.

And in all fairness, I have to tell you that the guy you hit is okay. Bruised and sore, and probably facing some hospital bills he doesn't deserve, but okay. I've talked to him a couple of times.

He'd really like to find you. I don't blame him. Life is unfair sometimes.

I just wanted you to know. Maybe you have no memory of this. Maybe you woke up the next morning, wondering how you got home. Maybe you went outside and found a small dent in your car. Maybe you swore to yourself never to do it again. Maybe you were grateful that you didn't hurt yourself or somebody else.

Maybe you'll read this, and think about that some more.

Father To The Man

I knew there was a metaphor around here somewhere.

I've been looking for it lately, sensing it skulking around. I even spent three hours cleaning the garage the other day, finding two screwdrivers and six pairs of work gloves, but no answers.

I was looking for something specific. Something that would explain what's going on, why and what I feel and how it all fits and makes sense.

I found a Soloflex in my garage, too. I knew it was there, hidden under the sleeping bags. It was a present to myself when I was 32 and making a lot of money, a debt I owed my inner teenager. Finally I'd get muscles; I could afford them now.

That's what I wanted when I was 15. Muscles. Muscles and a beard. There were other things I wanted, but I was a practical kid and muscles and a beard were a good start.

I was in my room, lifting weights that summer, the summer of 1974 I think, when my dad stopped by to watch. I was on my last set of bench presses, 110 pounds X 10 X 3. The ninth rep was a struggle. The tenth wasn't happening.

So Dad spotted me. He came in and helped me get the barbell up and on the stand, and while I breathed hard and strutted a bit, he stared at the weights, thoughtfully.

I have a son, so I know. Fathers and sons are complicated, but there are life lessons that only a man can teach a boy.

My dad picked up the barbell, tested it a moment, as if for balance, and then lifted it over his head like a feather. He set it down gently, sort of grunted, and then left the room.

He did this with one hand, by the way. In case I missed the point.

They say that sons will always find something that their fathers did and do it better. The rule never applied to me; there was nothing my father did, no avocation or hobby or chore, that I can come close to, so I don't try. I stay away from power tools and home improvement projects. My Soloflex stays in the garage, gathering dust. I will never be as strong.

But I'm stronger than I was. There's some order to my life now. Check stubs tell me I'm still productive. The scale tells me I'm doing all right for a guy my age. The mirror gets a little whimsical sometimes, but mirrors are like that.

In some ways, like so many people, I've grown into middle age to find life waiting for me, giving proof to George Eliot's maxim: It's never too late to become what you might have been. And as I've tried to figure out just exactly what that was, over these past eight months I've watched my father slip away.

I watched him battle through the nausea and lethargy, through the chemotherapy and radiation, waiting for the good days that would come. The doctors said there would be good days.

Doctors can be wrong, though.

Cancer knocks at the door one day, out of the blue, with a new and all together different product. It's called The Future, and what once was vague and undefined is now crystal-clear and sharp, if ephemeral. Cancer is the salesman for mortality.

Pneumonia closes the deal.

My father died in his sleep on Thursday, December 11, four days after his 67th birthday. He was the strongest man I ever knew. I am, in many ways, a poor imitation of him, but we were different people. Some things rubbed off, too.

Never buy cheap tools, he taught me; that's one time when you get what you pay for.

Take care of your teeth, he told me. Cherish your family. Work hard.

Seek out your happiness, he said. Life's not long enough to wait for it.

"I'm as weak as a kitten," he complained to me a few days before he died, and then told me his plan to get out to his workshop and cobble together some sort of device to help strengthen his legs. He would have, too. Just waiting for a good day.

I look back now and realize that, for whatever reason, as his strength ebbed mine was cresting. Suddenly I have my metaphor.

It's toward the end of the movie. The doctors are working on both of them, and then the boy screams and the bond is broken. Elliott's vital signs start improving, and E.T. begins to die.

Sometimes you can't pick your metaphors, by the way. Sometimes they pick you.

This is the last lesson we teach our sons. The ties will eventually go slack and we're on our own, and if we're not ready then tough. We can only hope we've learned enough by watching, because our spotters have moved on. I can lift my own weight now, but it will never give me a break, and I know it will never go away.

GenÜflection

I spent the better part of last night's "West Wing" trying to explain to my son the history of nuclear proliferation, which is the sort of quality time we cherish and why he is running away from home soon.

It's hard enough, I would think, to be 14 without getting impromptu lectures by Dad on geopolitics. When I was a kid, if I asked a simple question while my parents were watching TV, I'd be told to look it up. Or to shut up, depending on whether or not it was "The Big Valley." Both of which are parental options with merit, especially the first, considering that he has all the information he could use at his fingertips 10 feet away from the TV at the computer, but no. I had to let my inner nerd come out to play.

In all fairness, I was probably inspired by another really, really boring episode of my favorite show, something NBC is getting good at producing (February Sweeps motto: "Oh, You'll Watch It Anyway"). So I droned on about the Manhattan Project and Hiroshima and John probably regretted giving up an hour of playing Star Fox for this and it occurred to me that we exploded a couple of big bombs in 1945 and then everyone went home and made babies.

I knew this, of course. It was just an odd juxtaposition. The Bomb and Boomers.

I've been thinking a lot about my particular generation lately. I recently made an interesting discovery, which I can't exactly verify but I read it on the Internet so it must be true (I have money coming from Nigeria any day now). Tucked inside the biggest demographic bump of the last century, this group of us born between 1946 and 1964, is a nice little spike: In 1957 and 1958, more babies were born than before or after.

I pointed this out to my friend Rita the other night, whom I refer to as Lovely Rita behind her back for a reason all Boomers can figure out. Rita is my age, 45, born in 1958, and she didn't know we were special, either.

We are the ÜberBoomers, then, Generation Ü, the youngest people on the planet who remember when Kennedy was killed, born a little too late for Sesame Street and draft cards, virgin voters in 1976, just watchers in the 60s when our older brothers and sisters got to protest and take their clothes off and have all the fun. We think of Adam West as the one and only Batman. We were already in bed when the first episode of "Star Trek" aired. We are drifters in a generation chock full of icons and Special Bulletins, stranded somewhere between Vietnam and video games, and we have absolutely no chance of getting Social Security.

I'm not going to talk about disco.

But there are a lot of us, apparently, so I say we get organized. We are automatically elite, after all; Bill Gates (1955) can't buy his way in and Tom Hanks (1956) can't charm us out of a membership. There is strength in numbers and we have very specific ones.

So it starts now, the Official ÜberBoomer Movement (do not say this fast). Our mission is to establish an official Gen Ü ideology, cause, and cultural identity marker (nobody suggest "Welcome Back, Kotter," please). And maybe our own Visa card, I don't know. I'm just thinking out loud here.

I'm nominating Kevin Bacon (July 8, 1958) as our chairman, because of the whole six degrees thing. Someone please tell Kevin.

The first step is to always read this column, every week, as there will be many updates on our progress unless I forget about this, which is likely. And we're not snobs; we welcome thoughts and advice from all of the non-Ü you. It's not your fault you can't come in the clubhouse. And maybe you wouldn't want to. It's not easy being Ü. There's the disco thing.

I'd be interested in finding more Übers, particularly famous ones. We're going to need some name recognition if this thing is going to get off the ground. I tried doing a quick search online by typing "tell me the names of famous people born in 1957 or 1958" but my computer made some strange noises and that Mr. Jeeves guy made motions like he was going to slit his throat, so I'll have to depend on the kindness of strangers.

Tom Cruise (1962) is out. So is Sen. John Edwards (1954), as much as might want to be a member. And I can't make an exception for Meryl Streep (1949) or Renee Zellweger (1969). So right now it's me and a few friends and Kevin Bacon. We need help.

So let's get with it, people. Atomic batteries to power, turbines to speed.

Did I mention that someone needs to tell Kevin? Thanks.

It's A Zoo Out There

With all the news lately, you might have missed this. It's an election year, after all, and Mel's movie is coming out and the Oscars are coming up and we actually had some sunshine here last week. There's still some sniffing going on about George W's service in the National Guard, whether he put in enough hours and how often he got his teeth cleaned, that sort of thing. It's hard to keep up with all that's going on, so I can see how this story could have slipped through the cracks a couple of weeks ago.

There are gay penguins in New York zoos.

I know what you're thinking. "Tell me something I don't know," you're saying.

I read this story in the New York Times, a respected newspaper that prints all the news that is fit, and then maybe some other stuff. Sometimes they print untrue things, but I gather they're working on that problem.

We shouldn't be all that surprised. After all, with the exception of Adam Sandler, most types of human behaviors have correlates in the animal kingdom. In fact, this very same article mentioned that homosexual activity has been documented in over 450 species, not to mention most sitcoms. There's nothing really new here. Except for the penguin part. There's your story.

My favorite joke concerns penguins, by the way. Two penguins (I don't know if they are gay; it doesn't matter) are standing on an ice floe. One says to the other, "You look like you could be wearing a tuxedo." The other one says, "What makes you think I'm not?"

This is a Rorschach joke, a keen indicator of one's sense of humor. If you laugh at it, which virtually no one does, then that tells us something about you, although I don't know what. All I know is that I howled the first time I heard it, and I'm smiling right now, too.

OK, sorry for the digression. Where was I? Something about penguins? Wait. Now I remember. I was talking about biology, and scientific observation, and culture wars and the sanctity of marriage. I just got off track for a second.

They were marrying like crazy in San Francisco, weren't they? People from all over the country just pored into the City by the Bay, anxious to say vows and take blood tests. Las Vegas still might be king of the spontaneous conjunction, but our neighbor to the south here is making some serious inroads.

Which is all well and good, you might say, if you're the kind of person who says things like, "All well and good." Commitment is nice, it's mature and responsible, it binds our social fabric or something along those lines. It's just, you know. You know.

We've got ourselves an issue. We'll look back on this eventually and try to put the pieces together. Was it Howard Dean, and his tacit approval of civil unions in Vermont? Was it the Massachusetts high court decision combined with San Francisco mayor Gavin Newsome's decision that banning gay marriage was a violation of civil rights? Or was it just time, an outgrowth of awareness and openness and frank discussion and the whole "Will and Grace" thing?

Whatever the genesis, we're talking about it now, and it's not going away. It's going to play some part in the upcoming presidential election, you can be sure. It's a thorny subject for politicians because, unlike penguins, gay people vote.

If you're a Republican, you don't want to appear intolerant, yet you have to remain true to your traditional values and don't want to make the Religious Right angry, and they're ALWAYS getting angry about something. If you're a Democrat, you want to be seen as more tolerant than the other guy but still not out of the mainstream, since most voters live in Mainstream, U.S.A. It's a puzzle and it requires finesse, unless you're willing to just say what you think and what you feel. Like that's going to happen.

I don't mean to be light and careless with a serious subject (actually, that's exactly what I mean to be, but I'm giving myself an out here). There are issues to be discussed, issues of rights and culture and the nature of marriage in our society. It's just that my mind's been made up for a while now on this issue.

I'm a big fan of marriage. I think it's an exercise in ambition, an act of incredible optimism and hope. I think weddings are quixotic, battling against common sense that says that people change over time and commitments soften. There are marriages of convenience and marriages of passion, and everything in between. It's an ultimately selfless act, occasionally irrational and beautiful and individual, and so really none of my business.

You may disagree, of course. You may think it's all about your business, and you may make very good points, religious or otherwise. I've certainly heard some.

But don't tell the penguins. They just want to be left alone.

The Rummage Sale

I took a shortcut the other day, and I ended up in the middle of lives.

I was just trying to leave the building, this maze of a church I attend. I know it fairly well, which is to say not very well at all, as it's stood for over a century and contains tiny hallways and nooks and crannies and narrow stairways and for all I know a Batmobile and Jimmy Hoffa. You need your wits about you to navigate in this place, and heaven help you if your mind wanders on your way out.

I decided to cut through a large dining hall in the basement, of which there are several in this church or maybe fifteen. It was dark and I had to wait for my eyes to adjust, and I found myself in the middle of 1000 square feet of memories.

It was a rummage sale, or one waiting to happen. There was danger everywhere; church rummage sales are minefields for dumb men who don't know any better. Hours and hours of work go into them, mind-numbing details and price stickers and organization, and you want to tread very carefully lest some lady your grandmother's age finds you wandering and touching stuff and decides to kill you then and there. They take it very seriously, and so do I.

So I just looked, walked slowly and observed, hoping I wouldn't get caught being where I didn't belong.

There were clocks and cookbooks, toys and games, clothes and what seemed like a thousand shoes. There were stories here, lurking on the tables, just waiting for some Pixar wizard to work his CGI magic and turn them into family entertainment, coming soon to a theater near you.

Rummage sales are different, it seems to me, than other repositories of old stuff, different from antique shops and junkyards and, for example, my closet. There seems to be a statute of limitations, as if people who give something away to raise money for a good cause have a sense of propriety. They don't dump on a church rummage sale, and so nothing seemed older than 20 years.

But that's still a trip, 20 years, one I wandered down for a few minutes. There were paperback books and board games and kitchen appliances with signs that said, "It Works!!" This was a time capsule of the early 80s or late 70s, and at the back of the room I saw it.

It was a behemoth of a VCR, big and bulky, a relic of an earlier age with a tuner that went up to 13 and that was far enough, thank you. It probably cost a thousand dollars and was useful for taping football games and Johnny Carson, that was about it; there were no video stores when this baby was new.

And it looked new still, pristine and without a price tag; maybe they'll auction it off, appealing to someone with a good memory and a sense of history and an appreciation for ancient electronics. Someone like me. Hide my checkbook now.

This wasn't about craftsmanship; there was nothing that appealed to a sense of work ethic or hinted of long hours in the making. It was just a metal box with buttons, but it made me think we've forgotten the magic.

It could be just my particular point in life, but I remember when technology seemed to be exploding all around, appealing to the kid in us and emptying our wallets for things we really didn't need, just to have it. There's a statement in there somewhere, about values and priorities and commerce and (probably) credit, but I still remember and miss the excitement.

Where's my computer? The first one, 15 years ago, with that mighty 286 processor and 40 megabyte hard drive that I'd never, they assured me, ever fill up, and a staggering 1 meg of RAM just for emergencies. It was a workhorse, a DOS dynamo with a black-and-white monitor, and it could crunch numbers (sort of) and word process (after a fashion) and even make sounds (if you call it that). I started a business with it and my kids learned on it, and I want to know where it is.

I bought a new one a couple of weeks ago, a laptop that I can now haul around and send instant messages to my daughter in Texas on while I'm lying in bed, which tells you more about the quality of my life than I really want you to know. It's sleek and fast and fun, and in a couple of years it'll feel slow and bulky and one day it'll go too, become a doorstop or another item gathering dust, and I will have forgotten again.

Oh, it's just a thing, a dumb thing, I know. There is sunshine and family and books and neighbors, all to be cherished and appreciated. It's just that I got lost the other day, rummaging through reminders of other times, and somehow I remembered when things were new and exciting.

This is why we have eBay, I guess, and church rummage sales. You wander down the aisles and check prices and imagine histories. Maybe you'll run across an old VCR, or a computer with a big box and an oversized keyboard, a balky processor and virtually no software. It might be mine. It might be somebody else's.

But I'm willing to bet that, in some way, somebody probably would like it back.

Thank Heaven...

I forget sometimes that they can be so small. They were tiny, hobbits, brownies, baby Girl Scouts and they had cookies to sell and they had me at hello.

I bought Thin Mints. For my wife. I'm not a cookie person.

But they give me pause, these little girls. I tread very carefully. "I would love to buy some cookies," I say, but that's the extent of my personality. I'm polite but I don't joke with them and I certainly don't touch them, although I want to. I want to pat their heads and hold their hands, talk to them about their teachers and their pets and some of their favorite things, but I am a very appropriate person. Besides, Mom is always there, watching, smiling and pleasant but cautious; you can never be too careful. So I just hand over my money and say thanks and they'll never know what I was thinking.

I used to have a little girl, just like you.

I'm not whining or getting sappy here, by the way. It was just a moment, and it passed. Just another day in this purgatory that passes for the lives of fathers whose girls grow up. We get thoughtful and watch from a distance, remembering and wondering how it can be that our best days, out of all of them, were not spent in high school or college or in wooing our wives or building careers but in being daddies to little girls. Not fair.

Like anything is.

So I'm not sad, or even sentimental at the moment. No need to worry. And my girl is home this week, a quick trip for spring break, and then six weeks later she settles in for the summer, finds a job and learns how to drive all over again and complains that there is no food in the house ("There is NO FOOD IN THIS HOUSE!"), and then she really will be gone. They love her in Texas, apparently, love her talent and her brains and her spirit, and they will keep her and so will the world. And I will buy more cookies.

It's just that you think you know us.

You make your jokes. We can't cook or dress ourselves or pick our underwear off the floor. These are sexist stereotypes but stereotypes come from somewhere. There is truth here, and fairness. We men got our way for a long time. We built bridges and cleared forests, but somehow over the years a little more body mass and dense muscle tissue has become redundant, or even unnecessary other than moving the occasional couch.

You can make fun of us now; it's only fair and right. We got good at killing deer for dinner but over millennia we forgot to go to graduate school, so now you can make jokes and put up with us and love us and accept us and you still don't know.

You sigh and roll your eyes. You think we are channel hopping through life, searching for naked bodies or blood or adventure. You think we're trying to re-live old glories or find new ones. You think we're still trying to impress the other men, or the new woman at the office. We are all strut and cockiness, you think, an embarrassment to ourselves. You suspect we might be still searching for the perfect Playmate or soul mate, against all odds.

And some of us are like that, of course. And some of us are creeps, or freaks, or worse. In all fairness.

But some of us are just searching for our daughters. And waiting for them to come home.

We want to teach them all over again, tell them all we know, all we've learned in locker rooms and boardrooms. We want to teach them about the phases of the moon and the merits of the West Coast Offense, teach them about bad and indifferent and all in between, and then make them Sloppy Joes for dinner and watch "Sleeping Beauty" for the umpteenth time and remember that it only takes a kiss to wake.

As I say, I'm not sitting here weeping at the keyboard. I've adjusted, the way we adjust. I know I'm in the in-between stage, not quite old enough to be grandfatherly but certainly past my young father period. I just was reminded the other day.

My girl has been gone for a long time. We communicate through email and IMs and free long distance, but it's not the same. It's not like it used to be, when she'd hold my hand and we'd walk. Now she walks by herself and that's cool, that's appropriate. And I'm left here, and you can make your jokes.

But I saw a little girl the other day, and I realized I have always seen her. She sells cookies, she giggles, she wonders about life, she is wary, and she is my love, oh that she knew she were.

The Message

I got a package from my mother on Saturday. It had her return address on it, but of course I recognized the handwriting.

My handwriting is awful. It's worse now, after years on a keyboard, but it was always lousy. I have report cards from elementary school with A's in all other subjects but a big fat C in penmanship. I was hopeless.

It's a lost art, probably, left to the esoterically inclined. Like doing your own taxes, or tune-ups. We can still, most of us, do simple calculations in our head without benefit of microchips, but when the power goes out God forbid we have to write something.

Handwriting analysis aside, which I know nothing about, it's easy to do a little carbon dating when reading someone's penmanship. My mother's is of a different time, when it was an important subject and spoke to the world of character.

I remember my grandmother's handwriting, and her sister's. Both would send me letters when I was away in college, and both seemed interchangeable. Years later, I edited our church newsletter and ladies of a certain age would mail me items for submission, and I recognized the handwriting. I'd open up the envelopes and almost expect a five-dollar bill to come out, it was that familiar.

In the package from my mother was a small, rectangular box with "Tiffany's" on the top. There was also a note, and on the outside of the envelope she wrote something that made me laugh out loud.

"This is not from Tiffany's."

It was my father's pen. He carried it for years, so long that he'd burnished the gold plating and worn off his engraved name on the cap. I can barely make it out. It's my name, too.

I didn't think about asking for something of his when I was home for the funeral. It seemed an empty ritual, somehow a negation of the 45 years that rattle around in my brain. Mom gave my son his watch, which was a good thing; he wears it sometimes, and sometimes keeps it on his desk where he can look at it and remember his grandpa. I have lots to remember, though. I knew him longer.

But I have this pen now. It was his work pen, the one he slipped in his pocket every morning before heading off. He was an orthotist, a maker of braces, a craftsman. He probably wrote instructions and prescriptions with it, and drew diagrams and schematics.

He was old-fashioned, believing in quality work and frustrated with the way his field changed over the years. Materials got shoddy and cheap, and mass production seemed the way of the future and the patients suffered. I don't think his last 10 years before retirement were particularly happy ones.

I understand this. Lately I've been wondering if sitting in front of a computer all day isn't a waste of life. I find myself thinking sometimes, it's time to get a real job. Where you leave the house in the morning and come back in the evening, get a paycheck on time and do, in a perfect and just world, something you enjoy doing. Something that feels right. Something that feels like a job.

All of this was on my mind when I opened the package and took out the pen. I tried to picture it in his hand, tried to remember, tried to associate it somehow, but I couldn't. It was just a pen. Nice to have, though.

So this was also a good thing. Something to show my grandchildren, maybe, as I tell them about their great-grandfather, what he did and who he was. Maybe I'd tell them about his little lists of chores, which for some reason is my particular memory of him. Those Saturday lists, stuck on the refrigerator, carefully printed out in block letters, crossed off one at a time. Why I think about that, I don't know, but I do.

Then I picked it up and tried it out, to see if it still worked, and it took my breath away.

It was the ink, of course, or the shape of the point or just my imagination, but I wrote my name and it was his name and his hand. The writing was firm and strong. I wouldn't write like that in a million years.

I don't understand any of this.

I haven't tried it again. I slipped it into my notebook, the one I keep to make notes for myself. Things to remember. Things to do.

It waits for me now, my father's pen. I can speculate all I want on inanimate objects, on echoes of a life that resonate through ordinary things. I can be as goofy as anybody else. But I know what I saw.

And I know what I'll do. Someday soon, when I'm ready, when I'm frustrated or energized or desperate enough, I'll take his pen and I'll make a list.

It'll be in careful, crisp block letters, and I know that somewhere on it will be a job for me to do. Which my father could have told me, of course, and did. And is.

The Quality of Mercy

My grandmother cried when Elvis died, I remember. Just wept. My grandmother. Elvis.

It's funny how we react, hearing the news that a famous person has passed on. Their lives get tangled up with our own, mixed in with memories. Our first date, our first vote, the first time we fell in love at the movies. We mark moments, we speculate on whether they really do die in threes as our mothers claim, we watch a retrospective and read an obituary, and we have stories.

I have a story.

It was announced last week that Mercedes McCambridge had died, at age 87. A celebrity to be sure, an Oscar-winning actress for "All The King's Men," and after a fading career she had perhaps her biggest fame as the voice of the Devil in "The Exorcist." She had the voice for it, for sure.

A Life, then, as the Irish say. And oh, she was Irish.

She was also my friend, for a very short time, what seems like a very long time ago.

"I didn't believe a word of it!" was the first thing she said to me. We were in rehearsal for Sam Shephard's "Buried Child," a play she despised. She wasn't all that happy with my monologue at the moment, either.

I was playing her husband, hard enough when you're 23 and your co-star is 40 years older, but then I imagine it was never easy being her husband.

She was loud and bossy, and I don't think she particularly cared to be in the boonies of Northern Arizona, working with students, doing plays she didn't like. But it was a job, and it was acting, and acting was what she knew. And she knew it, trust me.

Early on, she twisted her ankle on a cable backstage while we were doing "Blithe Spirit." It didn't seem to improve her mood, and she spent the rest of the summer in a wheelchair mostly, griping and snapping at anyone who got in her way. I hid a lot.

We hated her.

And then, one day in rehearsal, she needed a prop, a liquor bottle. One of the crew dashed off to the office of our technical director, a gin drinker, and found an empty in a trash can. It was filled with water and rushed to the stage, and Mercedes McCambridge poured and drank. And stopped.

She smiled then, a small smile and a strange sight for us, after all these weeks. She looked at the glass, and looked at us.

"My God," she said. "I haven't tasted gin in years."

And she began to talk.

We knew, I suppose, something of her battles with alcoholism. It was part of her resume, her story, and there were long bouts and many hospitalizations, and finally AA and recovery. She talked of this, and also of Joan Crawford and Jack Kennedy,

Marlon Brando and Orson Welles. Movies she'd made and places she'd been, and for an hour or so we sat at the feet of our enemy and listened.

She broke character that day, and we saw a life, and we learned something.

Her friends called her Mercy. I called her Ms. McCambridge, of course.

On opening night of "Buried Child," we had a dialogue, she and I. Ms. McCambridge was offstage, reading from her script, while I sat alone on a couch. It was a difficult trick, lines and lines of one-word sentences and interjections, and at some point I flubbed. She covered, I covered, and we went on.

Afterward, she pulled me aside. "Young man, you were a pro out there," she said, a pro being what she was and what she respected most of all.

She talked to me, then, from time to time, gave me suggestions and praised me occasionally. She encouraged a career, which never happened but then I was young and she was a famous person. I listened.

I never saw her after that summer, never crossed her path again, but I was glad for the experience and grateful that I'd survived. I'd never met a tougher woman, or a better actress, and I say that knowing it's true and knowing it would be a compliment to her.

I followed what remained of her career, noted her biographies and caught her old movies when I could. I saw her on "Magnum, P.I." one night, playing a washed-up actress, the villain, wheelchair bound until the end, when she leapt from the chair and tried to escape.

At the end of the show, Magnum explained. It seems she'd twisted an ankle during a production of "Blithe Spirit," he said, and was in a wheelchair and just loved the attention it gave her.

I knew this already, of course, knew that she loved the spotlight and being theatrical and living up to her reputation. It was quite a reputation, all earned, and when I heard the news, heard that she'd died on March 2 but the announcement was made on St. Patrick's Day, I knew who was responsible, and why.

One Particular Spring

I have been chasing after moments my entire life.

I want to snag them, slap them in some amber and study them. I want to know what will happen, what might, what could, what did. I am a temporal archeologist, looking for answers in slivers of time.

There's a subjunctive sense about part of this; I look at a particular moment and wonder if it will mean something someday, and what. But we can't, we can't know, we can't have any idea at all, so mostly I just look back, see how it all turned out, and hope maybe I'll learn something.

I'm not talking about choices, although choices are important. The decisions we make in life, though, are tempered by a lot of things, among them our sense of morality, and fear. Keep the baby, take the job, return the wallet, hold your tongue: Minor or major, these are the choices we make that send us spinning down life.

But there are other moments when things happen, coincidences and random encounters and just odd things, and those are the times I like to look at and remember, and wonder about. And lately I've been thinking about Butch.

His name was Allen, but we called him Butch and I don't know why. He was, among other things, an actor. He was a big man, tall with broad shoulders and huge hands, and movie star looks. If he had been born 30 years earlier, I could see Butch in those

1950s epics, driving chariots or scaling castle walls. He had an epic look.

His best friend was Paul, who happened to be my best friend, so it was an uneasy relationship at times. We tended to circle each other, a little wary. Still, we were friends of a sort, and then one day he did me a favor.

I'd left college for three years, trying some adventures and then working to earn enough money to return. At the end of my first year back, my savings were history and I needed a job, and this is where Butch came in.

He'd worked the summer before at a dinner theater, and even though by this point Butch had left town, heading for bigger dinner theaters and, we assumed, eventually Hollywood, he came back for visits and that spring he decided I should take his old job.

I've written about this little dinner theater before; it was a nice gig for college students, steady pay and fun, but singing and dancing weren't exactly jumping out from my resume. So Butch had to twist my arm a bit.

He drove up the morning of the auditions, hovering around me like a mother hen, giving me advice, telling me to relax, making sure I had my music, and whispering in the ear of the director from time to time. Whether or not this made the difference, I don't know; Butch said I did it myself. I think I probably got some help.

The job was mine, though, and I had a good summer and I met a cast member and fell in love, and so on. My life would have been different, no question. So I owe Butch one.

A couple of weeks later, Butch came back into town for a visit. He and Paul went to a restaurant and sat in the bar, talking and drinking. In the dining room, a young woman was having dinner with someone she really didn't want to be with, much less be seen with. She got up to leave, finally, and now I have my moment.

I wasn't there, by the way. I can still see it.

The young woman heads for the door, glad to be done with an awkward dinner. She passes the bar on her way, and Butch sees her. He's met her a couple of times, knows her slightly, and he calls out.

Butch is not someone she wants to see, either, at this particular moment. So she ignores him and keeps walking. Paul is not paying attention to any of this.

This is where I freeze the frame, and tell you what would happen, and why I take this moment out from time to time to look at, and wonder about.

A few months later, Paul would move to Seattle. He'd call me and describe the Northwest in glowing terms, and I'd eventually follow him out here.

The young woman heading for the exit would, in a year or so, stand one day on a hill overlooking the red rocks of Sedona, and marry me.

And later that night, after leaving the restaurant, Butch would fall asleep at the wheel on a desert highway and die.

It's just a moment, I know. A chance encounter between three people whose lives and actions were and are inextricably bound with mine, on a pivotal night. A moment that now belongs to me.

Looking back, I have great affection for all three of these young people, and for that one particular spring. Paul is still my friend. My wife is still my wife.

And Butch is now forever young, reminding me and others of a spring of change, when most of us had lots of life to yet live, and one of us didn't, and none of us, of course, had any idea at all.

This Perfect Day

For his 67th birthday, I sent my father a book about the history of the Los Angeles Dodgers. When I spoke to him on the phone, he seemed a little puzzled.

"But I don't like the Dodgers."

I didn't try to explain much; talking on the phone then was hard for him. He had almost no voice and ran out of oxygen fairly quickly. I just hoped that he'd get a chance to look through the book and maybe understand why I'd sent it, but there wasn't enough time. He passed away four days later, maybe never understanding that my intention was to remind him that I always listened to his stories.

He was a fan of the Dodgers in the 1960s, when he lived in Southern California. I'd talk to him about this sometimes, trying to find one more connection, this time baseball. I'd ask a lot about Sandy Koufax, a mystery man to me, a stunning pitcher who quit in his prime rather than risk the injury he saw coming.

I thought maybe the pictures from those days and those teams would be nice for him to look through.

I'm not really good with gifts.

We did make a baseball connection, though, finally. After he moved on to other sports, mostly football, in the spring of 2001 my parents moved from New Mexico to Arizona for retirement, and Arizona, it turned out, now had a baseball team. So Dad watched.

Trying to explain passion for baseball to someone not interested is like trying to explain algebra to a 3-year-old; they see your mouth moving and hear the words, but that's about it. A six-month season divisible by 154 meaningless but eventually important games, little gains and little losses, a game made for radios in the garage while you're doing something else.

And, if you're fortunate, if you love a team and follow them regularly, at least once in your life you'll experience an honest-to-God pennant chase, when baseball rises to another level and antacids are in order.

Mariners fans got this for the first time in 1995, our first glimpse of hope, our first whiff of October in August. I went to the first playoff game in Mariner history, sitting behind the bullpen, watching Randy Johnson warm up to face the Yankees. We were down 0-2 in a five-game series, but we were home and we had Randy. We won, we won the next one, and then in Game 5, when things were tight and everything was on the line, with our pitching collapsing and the end in sight, everyone looked toward left field. There, on two days' rest, walking toward the mound, was The Big Unit. And we won, Edgar Martinez hitting a double deep and Ken Griffey scoring from first, and I was done. They didn't make the Series and I didn't care; I'd had my baseball moment.

I'd watched Randy Johnson for years, watched him as a 20-something wild man, a tremendous fast ball but not much else, whose strike-outs were matched by his walks, and saw him grow into what he would become. I watched him pitch a no-hitter in 1990 and saw him get close other times, including one nearly perfect game. Afterwards, he was calm.

"I'm not a perfect pitcher," he said.

We eventually lost him, sad but grateful. And my dad got him, and we had another connection.

As I say, you can only hope that once in your life you get a chase, a spectacular season. In 2001, the year my parents moved to Arizona, in his first season back to baseball, his new team, his newly acquired interest in this strange but wonderful game, my dad got a champion on his first try. The Arizona Diamondbacks won the World Series, and he became a believer in Randy Johnson.

So I've been thinking a lot about Dad lately, since hearing the news last week. At the age of 40, 14 years after his first no-hitter, Randy Johnson pitched a perfect game.

A few years ago, back when he was still a Mariner, Randy lost his father, and he began a tradition. When he wins a game, he points toward the sky. This is for you, Dad As he did Tuesday night.

It's been five months since my father died. Grief turns to something else in five months, begins to mellow, settles in for the long haul. There are moments, though, when I still want to reach for the phone.

I apologize to those of you who aren't interested in baseball who've read so far. I would only say that it's not all about baseball.

It's also about fathers and sons, complicated relationships, struggles to find something in common, and finding it, maybe, in simple things. A 98 MPH fastball. A whiff of a bat. A giant of a man, thrusting his arm toward the heavens, remembering his father. I remember mine, too. All the time, but particularly on a Tuesday night last week, when, for a few hours, Randy Johnson was finally a perfect pitcher.

www.ingramcontent.com/pod-product-compliance
Lightning Source LLC
Chambersburg PA
CBHW060821050426
42453CB00008B/525